HIDDEN
HISTORY
of
ROCHESTER
MINNESOTA

HIDDEN
HISTORY
of
ROCHESTER
MINNESOTA

Amy Jo Hahn

THE
History
PRESS

Published by The History Press
Charleston, SC
www.historypress.com

First published 2022

Manufactured in the United States

ISBN 9781467149532

Library of Congress Control Number: 2022936633

CONTENTS

ACKNOWLEDGEMENTS

As with my previous book *Lost Rochester, Minnesota*, I'm indebted to the wonderful staff and volunteers at the History Center of Olmsted County in Rochester, Minnesota, for their help in creating the captivating stories within these pages. Archivist Krista Lewis generously allowed me unlimited access to the history center's amazing archival resources, which includes subject and biographical files, various periodicals and books and historic images. It was difficult to choose which photographs to select for publication—a very nice dilemma to have. Linda Willihnganz, Lee Hilgendorf and Sean Kettelkamp offered advice, shared topic ideas, answered questions and helped bring clarification on facts and other information. I enjoyed countless conversations with people as passionate as I am about local history and solving the conundrums that come along with stumbling on historic stories and photographs. We often joked about how we tend to be a little like Alice in *Alice In Wonderland*, going down rabbit holes and embarking on interesting adventures that either take us to the discovery of something extraordinary, unveiling fascinating stories and characters or, disappointedly, quite devastatingly so, uncovering nothing. The History Center of Olmsted County is a priceless resource for genealogists, historians and the general public. It's a hidden gem of a resource, of which many people still know nothing about.

I'd also like to thank my husband, Chris Sattler, for encouraging and supporting me and understanding when I needed time to binge research and write. This resulted in Chris entertaining our toddler, Finnegan, while I focused on crafting this project. I'm extremely grateful, and I know Finnegan had a blast with his dad!

Researching and writing this book during a pandemic was extremely challenging at times. Life has been anything but easy, as anyone can attest to, and each person has had their own stresses and battles to deal with. I'm very appreciative of the compassion and patience of my editor John Rodrigue as I navigated this uncertain and historically significant period, trying to maintain focus, keep positive, regain a life-work balance and adjust to and accept so much out-of-my-control change.

Preface

The narratives that compose this book shine a spotlight on a handful of the interesting characters, events and places that share a historical connection to Rochester. It is the goal of The History Press's Hidden History series to bring attention to historical subjects that have mostly existed in the background of previous published media and general discussion or completely lost over time, providing some much-deserved attention.

Although you may see a familiar name in these pages, I tried to craft my stories so they reveal a few unknown, unique and intriguing facts, giving a new perspective and offering a more permanent, exposed preservation. For example, much has been written and recorded about Civil War veterans Jacob Dieter and James George, but I give more focus to their wives, Martha Muir Dieter and Rhoda Pierce George, and how the war and the absence of their husbands affected them and their young children.

Mixed with the somewhat familiar are new discoveries, such as Elizabeth Taylor Greenfield, a famous Black opera singer known as the "Black Swan," who performed in the city for two nights in October 1863. Also unveiled are Sarah Wright Clark, Julia Cutshall and Stella Doran Cussons, whose interesting stories came to light during research I conducted on local suffrage activists for the History Center of Olmsted County's *The Onward March of Suffrage* exhibit. Due to the fascinating information unearthed about the people, activities and organizations involved in Rochester's suffrage journey, the chapter about suffrage comprises excerpts from the unpublished research report I wrote summarizing my discoveries about the passionate and dedicated efforts to achieve equal voting rights.

I hope you enjoy these tidbits of Rochester's "hidden" history. And there's more—so much more to discover.

1

Beginnings

The Driftless Area and Karst Topography

The city of Rochester, Minnesota, sits in Olmsted County, on the northwest edge of what is known as the Driftless Area. The acreage encompassing this geographical region belongs to southwestern Wisconsin, southeast Minnesota, northeast Iowa and northwestern Illinois. It is a unique area of geological interest due to its lack of glacial drift. The *Merriam-Webster Dictionary* defines *drift* as "a deposit of clay, sand, gravel and boulders transported by a glacier or by running water from a glacier." During the Last Glacial Period (LGP), North America experienced several episodic advancements and retreats of glaciers. However, these large ice sheet occurrences did not happen in the Driftless Area, leaving it bereft of drift.

As part of the Driftless Area, southeast Minnesota's landscape has distinct characteristics not seen in other parts of the state. It boasts beautiful deep river valleys cut between high, jutting, jagged, rugged, golden bluffs; steep hills topped with trees; acres of woods; a multitude of rock outcroppings; and hundreds of spring-fed streams, both above and underground. The area comprises karst topography, which contains several types of porous rock: limestone, sandstone, dolomite and gypsum. The area's large amount of limestone and sandstone comes from a buildup of several materials, including that of animals that once inhabited a prehistoric sea covering southern Minnesota. These stone varieties soften and dissolve easily when exposed to slightly acidic water. After water flows through the topsoil, it seeps into

A karst sinkhole in the Driftless Area. *Amy Jo Hahn.*

the hard lower bedrock layers to a natural underground drainage system. One major contributor to this drainage system is the area's collection of sinkholes, seen most often in Fillmore County. Thousands of sinkholes dot the landscape as a result of rain, snow and melting ice dissolving the soluable rock layer and causing the ground to collapse inward and downward, creating a deep indentation in the ground. Often, trees and other vegetation sprout up from the floor of the sinkhole. These distinct karst features are common scenes in fields, with tree branches seemingly jutting straight from the ground in large clumps, the trunks buried from view.

Over thousands of years, this drainage system has formed a cavernous subterranean level below the region's surface. The most notable of these caves are Mystery Cave and Niagara Cave in Fillmore County, which are available for public tours from May to October. In addition to naturally formed caves, the porous rock allowed people to create their own caves. One such cave exists on Rochester's old state hospital property, now Quarry Hill Park, which was carved out by patients in order to store food and other supplies for the hospital.

Although the Driftless Area is the common name bestowed on Olmsted County and its southern and southeastern county neighbors, the area is also referred to as the Paleozoic Plateau Section (PPL). According to the

Rochester State Hospital's manmade storage cave. *Amy Jo Hahn.*

The Driftless Area's Root River, known by the Dakota as the Hokah. *Amy Jo Hahn.*

Minnesota Department of Natural Resources, the PPL is "a rugged region of bluffs and valleys that is quite different from the rest of the state. Although originally a plateau underlain by rather flat-lying sedimentary rocks from the Paleozoic era, in the past ten thousand years, the landscape has been highly eroded and dissected by streams and rivers tributary to the Mississippi River, such as the Root, Whitewater, Zumbro and Cannon Rivers and their predecessors. The remains of the plateau are most evident on interfluves along the western edge of the section." The Iowa Geological Society describes it as follows:

> *The rugged, deeply carved terrain seen in the Paleozoic Plateau is so unlike the remainder of the state that the contrast is unmistakable, even to a casual observer....The most striking differences include abundant rock outcroppings, a near absence of glacial deposits, many deep, narrow valleys containing cool, fast-flowing streams and more woodlands. This spectacular high-relief landscape is the result of erosion through rock strata of Paleozoic age. The bedrock-dominated terrain shelters unusually diverse flora and fauna, including some species normally found in cooler, more northern climates.*

The strikingly beautiful Driftless Area, with its abundant natural resources, from fresh waterways to a variety of small and big game, including elk, was considered home to the Paleo-Indians and eventually the Dakota and Winnebago people before the arrival of white settlers.

THE DAKOTA AND THE WAZI OJU RIVER

The Dakota people considered Rochester and its surrounding area part of their home territory before the arrival of Eastern settlers following the 1851 signing of the Treaty of Traverse des Sioux. After agreeing to part with thousands of acres in southeast Minnesota, the Dakota were forced to relocate to reservation land that was established on a few acres on either side of the south bank of the Minnesota River. For a few years following the treaty, tribes continued to roam the area, most often the Wahpekute and the Mdewakanton. They hunted and fished, set up temporary camps and interacted with white immigrants.

Rochester resident James Bucklin helped provide care for a young Dakota girl sick with an unknown illness during the winter of 1854–55. Bucklin provided a short narrative of his experience with the Dakota and their presence along the Zumbro River in *History of Olmsted County* (1883, 637–39):

> *In the fall of 1854, about two hundred Indians camped on the river bottom east of the site of John M. Cole's old flouring mill. They remained there about six weeks, and during that time, four of their number, three males and one female, died from sickness....The bodies were buried on the bluff nearly west of the site where Cascade Mill now stands. There were, in all, eight bodies of deceased Indians buried there, and the spot has forever been known as the Indian burial ground....On the account of sickness referred to, the chief ordered removal to a new camping ground...about one mile south of the city of Rochester....In the spring, the Indians all left, and this was the last seen of the Sioux in the county.*

The bluff Bucklin refers to, Indian Heights, is located on one of the highest hills in the city. The city park's most eastern overlook offers a beautiful panoramic view of the Zumbro River, a waterway the Dakota called the Wazi Oju, and Silver Lake. Silver Lake, a man-made reservoir created during the U.S. government's massive public works program

A view of the Wazi Oju or Zumbro River, Indian Heights, circa the early 1900s. *History Center of Olmsted County.*

initiative during the 1930s, was created near the bend of the river where the Dakota's camp was located. Due to Indian Heights's high elevation, river view and sunrise vista, it was a considered sacred to the Dakota people and therefore was an ideal place to bury the dead. The deceased mentioned previously were most likely buried in shallow graves due to the hard layered stone beneath the topsoil. Reverend Samuel William Pond, who lived among the Minnesota Dakota as a missionary from 1834 to 1853, correlates this idea, writing about how the Dakota buried their dead in *The Dakotas or Sioux in Minnesota as They Were in 1834* (480):

> *The dead were interred…in shallow graves two or three feet deep. The graves were protected by picket fences or by setting a row of posts on each side of the grave, leaning against each other at the top over the grave, the ends of the grave being protected by upright posts. These posts were set up as a protection against wild beasts….The Dakotas selected elevated locations for burying places and commonly set up poles by the graves of*

those recently buried, with pieces of white cloth tied to the top like flags. Those streamers were left to flutter in the wind till worn out....High on scaffolding in winter months, when they were unable to break ground due to freezing....Best clothes, embroidered moccasins, wrapped body in blanket, wrapped bandages around the blanket.

Although no human remains have been discovered on Indian Heights, it's believed that over time, evidence of the burial ground vanished due to city development, quarry harvesting and the natural elements, specifically the deadly 1883 cyclone that tore through the city of Rochester, destroying not only buildings but also uprooting trees and wreaking devastation on the natural environment.

In addition to camping in the shadow of their sacred bluff, the Dakota people of this area favored a campsite along the Wazi Oju in Pine Island, about twenty miles north of Rochester. Although the river has been termed the Waziouja, a predecessor to its French name, Riviere des Embarras, with both names alluding to the buildup of tree and vegetation debris obstructing the river's many crooked turns and hindering smooth passage to the river's mouth, many historical references favor Wazi Oju or Wazi Ozu as the earliest recorded name. The campsite at Pine Island was so favored that

Cascade Mill's location on Cascade Creek, near its conjunction with the Zumbro River, a favorite area for Dakota encampments. *Amy Jo Hahn.*

Cascade Creek with Indian Heights in the background, a sacred location to the Dakota. *Amy Jo Hahn.*

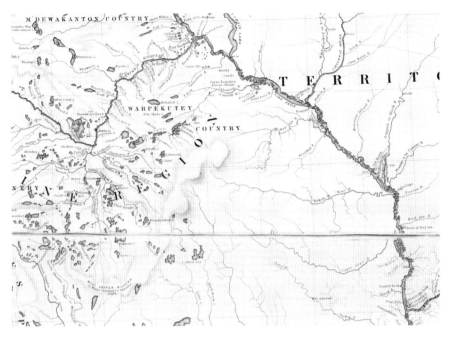

Southeast Minnesota Dakota names of rivers and territories in 1843. *Joseph Nicollet Map.*

the river was named after it. The name Wazi Oju, translates to "River of Pines"; it has also been called the Wapka Wazi Oju or Pines Planted River. The name pays homage to a large grove of tall, sentry-like white pine trees that once existed, providing needed shelter during the cold winter months. W.H. Mitchell wrote about this village in his 1869 *Geographical and Statistical Sketch of the Past and Present of Goodhue County* that "Between the two branches of the Zumbro River, which unite a short distance below, there was quite a forest of pine, which could be seen for a long distance over the prairie, giving it quite the appearance of an island in the sea" (118). A vivid description of the camp is given in the 1920 *Minnesota Geographic Names: Their Origin and Historic Significance* (288):

> *The island proper is formed by the middle branch of the Zumbro, which circles around the present village, enclosing a tract once thickly studded with tall pine trees....This spot was one of the favorite resorts of the Dakota Indians. They called it Wa-zee-wee-ta, Pine Island, and here in their skin tents, they used to pass the cold winter months, sheltered from the winds and storms by the thick branches of lofty pines. The chief of Red Wing's village told commissioners of the United States, when asked to*

sign the treaty that would require his people to relinquish their home on the Mississippi River, that he was willing to sign it if he could have his future home at Pine Island.

But the chief was not granted his request for the beloved Pine Island village, and the days of wintering at that location ceased to be. Eventually, the Dakota had no choice but to leave the river valleys, woodlands and grasslands of southeastern Minnesota, traveling further into the arid West, seeking land and food sources and distance from the seemingly unending migration of white settlers, vanishing from the landscape of the Driftless Area, a region they'd inhabited for countless generations.

Colonel George Healy and Rochester's First Cemeteries

When white immigrants from the east arrived in the territory that would become Rochester—the first among them being George Head and his family in July 1854—they faced a wilderness of woodlands and grasslands still frequented by the Dakota and Winnebago, even though they'd ceded the lands to the U.S. government. Eventually, the Native tribes disappeared from the landscape, as they were steadily forced to relocate farther west. Pioneers claimed their land, building homes, businesses, schools and churches, creating a frontier community that developed into a bustling and prosperous town. And as the people worked to develop a thriving community, something that was overlooked was a proper cemetery.

Colonel George Healy, a transplant from Cayuga County, New York, arrived in Rochester in 1859 and worked as a city surveyor for many years. He was raised by farmers in the town of Sennett, New York, and his parents were among its founding members. Healy pursued a career in engineering, and he worked as one of the chief engineers on the construction of the Erie Canal. He married Theodosia Polhemus in 1841 and had three children. Two of the children died before the family's relocation to Minnesota, and one of them died at the age of twenty-three in Rochester. It was perhaps this experience of devastating loss that spurred Healy's interest in creating a peaceful and beautiful resting place for Rochester's dead. Under his guidance and through his passionate dedication and generous donations, Rochester's most picturesque cemetery was designed and implemented: Oakwood Cemetery.

Colonel George Healy, a city surveyor and Oakwood Cemetery founder. *History Center of Olmsted County.*

Healy and Theodosia knew how important it was to have a tranquil place to visit a memorial to a loved one. It was no doubt incredibly difficult for them to not be near the graves of their children who were buried back in New York—so much so that when they buried their daughter Sarah "Dolly" in 1881, they included the names and dates of birth and death for their other children on the gravestone: George Polhemus, who died in 1846 at the age of three months, and Mary Amia, who died at the age of thirteen in 1856. It was mortifying for the couple to see bodies tossed into shallow unmarked graves in a plot of land between Cherry Street (Sixth Avenue Southeast) and Oakwood Street (Seventh Avenue Southeast). The first cemetery had no official name and existed on sandy ground on a small hillside surrounded by sparse trees designated as school property. People were buried and forgotten. No written records identifying them existed. Their families were left without a place to mourn. George and Theodosia weren't alone in their concern. Other residents found the lack of a respected cemetery appalling.

The editors of the *Rochester Post* wrote on December 1, 1860, that the discussion of a "city cemetery" was a "persistently-neglected subject," and "it cannot fail to touch the heart of every person who reads it, and to awaken a feeling of regret, not to say of shame, that thus late in the progress of a flourishing city there is not a 'God's acre' within or without its limits, sacred to all hearts as the resting place of the dead." The editors called on the city council to take up the matter immediately: "Will not the common council take a lead in this matter? Surely, the citizens will bear them out in whatever course they deem best to pursue in carrying forward so urgent and so necessary a public work." It was not the first time the editors stressed the importance of having a cemetery. With their call to action, they published a gorgeously written letter sent by "Myra":

> One beautiful day a fit of roving seized us, and we found ourselves on those pretty lands appropriated for school purposes; and ere we were aware, upon a place of graves. Our heart sank within us as we gazed on its utter desolation. Rank weeds and overgrown thistles contended for the mastery.
>
> No fence enclosed this ground, hallowed by tears and sacred as the last resting place of some of God's children. For the first time, we thought with regret of the home we had left, and sadly wending our way back, we thought, "Rochester may be a pleasant place to live, but God keep far from us the day when we shall die and be buried here!"
>
> Yes, we say, let us early select some fitting place to bury the dead, and make it beautiful; so when the last hours of life draw night for us, or for those who are dearer than self, there shall mingle with their solemnities, no dark thoughts of a dreary, desolate graveyard, overgrown with weeds, where cattle shall nip the scanty blades of grass from our grave, as fast as it shall spring up. Rochester is so rich in pretty, graceful bluffs, it seems to us there can be no difficulty in selecting a burial ground, that one of these days shall vie with Mount Auburn and Greenwood; of whose beauty and quiet shall almost seem inviting, to the world-worn and weary.

The letter's author references Mount Auburn Cemetery, which is located in Massachusetts between Cambridge and Watertown, and most likely Green-Wood Cemetery of Brooklyn, New York. Both were founded in the 1830s and considered "rural" or "garden" cemeteries. These types of cemeteries existed outside of crowded church graveyards within the confines of the city, offering several acres of open green space. These park-like resting places for the dead were given the name "cemetery." The word has Latin roots, referring to a "sleeping place." This was a departure from centuries of burying grounds only being associated with churches. Tall, stately, often uniquely and beautifully carved and crafted monuments take center stage among graveled pathways winding beneath large, lofty trees and through an immaculately manicured landscape. By 1863, the groundwork was laid for Rochester's own "green" cemetery when the Rochester Cemetery Association formed and forty acres were purchased. Oakwood Cemetery was built north of the original burial grounds, its entrance located on Seventh Avenue Northeast on the eastern side of the Zumbro River, with George Healy leading its development. The unidentified bodies from the first graveyard were transferred to the new cemetery, and every effort was made to recover all the bodies, but without documentation or markers, that goal was next to impossible. Afterward, every once in a while, a local newspaper would report a skeleton or skull surfacing in the location of the old graveyard.

The cemetery fast became a landmark of pride for the city's residents. A May 21, 1897 *Rochester City Post* article describes the beauty of Oakwood:

> *A cemetery is always looked upon by a stranger, as giving some clue to the moral tone of the community…for what respect shown to the memory of the departed, marks in a degree the esteem in which the living are held.… Oakwood Cemetery is one of the most beautiful of mementos to the departed loved ones. The green velvety grass that every where extends like a carpet throughout the ground, gives to the place an air of freshness, and with the trees of various varieties, numerous among which are the sturdy oak and the mournful pine, the effect is greatly enhanced, giving the added inspiration of a renewed life and vigor. The appearance of Oakwood cemetery, with its many beautiful flowerbeds of pansies, tulips and lilies in separate plots, and upon the graves of the dead, is a beautiful tribute to love…dear ones buried there, have the respect and veneration for their memories, which always keeps upon the graves some little touching tribute to their memory.*

Impressive monuments to the dead rose up from the green landscape. Among the most ornate and showy was the pink and gray mausoleum of George Washington Van Dusen, built during 1898. At the time, Van Dusen resided in Minneapolis, but he'd spent several years living in Rochester, where he started a prosperous business building grain elevators and warehouses along railroads. Despite his relocation, he loved Oakwood and wished to be entombed there. The structure was finished by winter, and the *Olmsted*

County Democrat wrote about the tomb in its December 8 issue, describing it as having been built in the Greek "Scipio Frieze" style, "acknowledged by artists and architects to be the finest in the world, with its channeled entablatures and metopes of the Doric order, extends around the entire building." The outside is made of gray granite, with columns of pink stone, the reception room and fifteen catacombs inside of Italian marble, as well as double front doors. The cost was reported to have been between $15,000 to $25,000. The paper wrote, "The finished work is the finest structure of the kind in the state, if not in any of the western states, and reflects great credit on the designer and contractor, Mr. J.M. Sullivan of Minneapolis, whose reputation in the line of fine memorial work has become national.… The Van Dusen mausoleum in Oakwood Cemetery is a gem of beauty and strength; a picture, chaste and symmetrical."

In addition to the Van Dusen crypt, another building takes center stage in the cemetery: the George Healy Memorial Chapel. Healy not only gave much of his time and talent to Oakwood, but he also provided financial support, including a gift of a receiving vault, which was presented in October 1890, and $75,000 was donated to the cemetery after Healy's

The G.W. Van Dusen crypt at Oakwood Cemetery. *Amy Jo Hahn.*

Oakwood Cemetery's George Healy Memorial Chapel. *Amy Jo Hahn.*

death in 1896. To honor Healy's contributions to Rochester's "White City," a chapel was built in his honor in 1912. The January 27, 1911 *Post and Record* described it as being "of Gothic design, standing about thirty-five feet high, about forty feet wide and fifty feet long. It will be built of Bedford cut stone with stained- or leaded-glass windows. A beautiful entrance forms the greater part of the front, on each side of which is a window, and overhead a large circle, which will also be stained-glass. One large and three small windows in harmony with architecture of the structure are on the sides. The ground plan forms a design of a cross." The chapel was fully renovated and restored in 2000.

Over its first several decades of existence, the cemetery's unassuming front entrance welcomed funeral processions, picnickers, Civil War veteran memorial parades, patriotic celebrations and mourners quietly visiting the resting places of loved ones. The cemetery grew to eighty-six acres by 1928, and in in the fall of 1929, a striking and majestic feature was added, signifying the cemetery's respected historical significance. A new front gate was erected in honor of Granville Woodworth, its $34,000 price tag funded by the bequest of Mary and Flora Woodworth, his daughters. Woodworth's Memorial Gateway rises twenty-five feet high and is thirty-

The George and Theodosia Healy family memorial at Oakwood Cemetery. *Amy Jo Hahn.*

Oakwood Cemetery's grand entrance, the Woodworth Memorial Gateway. *Amy Jo Hahn.*

three feet long, with a main entrance that is seventeen feet wide and sixteen feet tall. Tucked on either side are six-foot-wide pedestrian entrances and sloping sides that wing out with eight-foot-high and one-hundred-foot-long walls. A bronze plaque on the gate's west side recognizes the cemetery's first board of directors, which includes George Healy. He and Theodosia, who died in 1882, are among the nineteen thousand people buried in Oakwood, their monument a touching dedication to a loving couple. George possessed a modern belief that there were two heads of household, a man and woman, a husband and wife. It was common for tombstones to consist of one spire, in respect of the patriarch of the family, but George insisted on having something unique. Two-columns of granite rise from the stone base and merge at the apex of a pointed arch, ascending together into a single tall spire, in respectful honor of his wife, a woman he considered an equal life partner.

2

THE CIVIL WAR

MARTHA MUIR DIETER: A SOLDIER'S WIDOW

The fate of Civil War veteran Jacob Dieter has developed into a sort of local mystical tale. Some facts are known about his time spent as a Union soldier, while others conflict, confuse and collide. He was mustered into the Ninth Minnesota Volunteer Infantry, as part of Company F, on August 20, 1862, at Fort Snelling and was stationed in the southwestern part of the state, fighting the Dakota during the United States–Dakota War. In the fall of 1863, his regiment headed south to engage the Confederate army in a series of battles. Confederate forces captured Dieter in northern Mississippi on June 10, 1864, at the Battle of Brice's Cross Roads, commonly known as the Battle of Guntown. For a few days, it was not known exactly what happened to Jacob. Two weeks later, he wrote a letter to his family, confirming his capture along with fifteen other men from Company F, and he said he was being held at the notorious Andersonville Prison. He wrote, "Dear Wife and Children, I will write a few lines to you to let you know that I am well and hope this finds you all in good health....I send my love to you all."

But what happened to him after he penned this letter is unclear. Did he die in a Confederate prison, as government paperwork claims? Did he meet his end in a hospital, as reported in an 1870 *Rochester Post* article? Or did he escape during a rumored transfer to another prison and disappear into another life? There are unanswered questions when it comes to what happened after the Battle of Guntown, but regardless, he never returned home. And that is where the story ends for most, but what about his

Martha Muir Dieter. *History Center of Olmsted County, Crowell Portraits (Rochester, MN).*

family? He had a wife, Martha, and five children, one of whom was a newborn he never met. His absence left Martha, a single mother, facing the overwhelming challenge of figuring out how to secure financial means for her family's survival— no small feat for a woman during that time. But Martha had no choice. Her family's survival depended on her.

Martha Muir was born in Scotland on August 24, 1824, immigrating to the U.S. at the age of eighteen. She met and fell in love with the handsome, dark-haired, dark-eyed Jacob Dieter and married him at Fond du Lac, Wisconsin, on July 21, 1850. They lived in Wisconsin for a few years before moving to Olmsted County's Haverhill Township. Babies came quickly, and the young couple lived in a log cabin. Farming was Jacob's profession, and he hauled loads of harvested grain by oxen along the forty-mile stagecoach trail connecting Rochester to Lake City, since Rochester didn't have a railroad until 1864. It was a hard life, and money was a struggle. When there was a call from the U.S. Army for more soldiers, Jacob expressed his desire to serve, telling his family it was his duty. A steady military paycheck was also an attractive incentive. Their daughter Mattie recalled how her mother cried after her father's announcement. Having a husband on the warfront and being left at home to fend for herself were most likely terrifying prospects. Martha's tears and protests couldn't keep Jacob from enlisting. A few months after his enlistment, Jacob sent a letter requesting that Martha and the children visit him at Fort Ridgely northwest of Mankato. The army allowed men to have their families visit if the women agreed to cook, do laundry and other various chores for small compensation. Not wanting to pass up the chance to see Jacob and earn extra money, Martha packed up her household and traveled across a territory war-torn by skirmishes between the Dakota and the U.S. military. She entered the war zone of the United States–Dakota War.

It was a brave journey for a woman and young children, but Martha was a determined woman. Her daughter Martha, called Mattie, recounted the dangerous trip taken in a covered wagon in her 1927 recollections: "I remember when we went through the Mankato Woods over a log road, a man came on horseback to warn us from the Indians. We saw many skeletons; we passed a house where all the family had been killed except the husband. He got away in a cornfield." The family continued on, despite the dreary and frightening landscape, looking forward to being reunited with their patriarch. But upon their arrival at the fort, they were told they couldn't come inside due to an outbreak of smallpox. The family pitched a tent outside the fort and lived on the windswept prairie for three weeks, exposed to a Dakota attack, save one guard that was there to protect them. Eventually, they reunited with Jacob, who was residing in a brick house within the fort's high walls. Mattie wrote of swimming in a deep ditch that encircled the fort's perimeter, viewing buffalo and harvesting and eating plums while her mother worked hard, baking and cooking, sewing and mending, washing and cleaning. On top of worrying about the arrival of a Dakota war party, Martha experienced a scare when a bolt of electricity from a lightning strike singed her and the children's feet, leaving her unable to talk for two weeks and permanently damaging her hearing. According to Mattie, this harrowing incident occurred while Martha was at the stove. "The lightning strike traveled along a clothesline and down the broken lightning rod to the stove pipe." In the fall of 1863, at the end of the allotted three months, the army expelled Martha and the children. It was a heartbreaking parting. "I remember the tears that were shed when we parted from my father," recalled Mattie. Not long after the bitter parting, the family saw Jacob one more time during a two-week furlough. It was the last time they saw him. His regiment received their new orders. They were headed south. And Martha was left alone again.

Finances were a struggle for the Dieter family. Jacob inquired in letters if Martha received his thirteen-dollar-a-month pay, even asking in his last letter if the money he postmarked in Saint Louis had arrived. He also wrote that Martha should ask his parents for help if she found herself in need. Martha had her hands full at home and depended on the Union funds to get by, but when Jacob landed in prison the checks stopped. Martha was in a constant state of worry, about her husband, paying her bills, having enough food to eat and about her small children, who suffered bouts of severe croup and scarlet fever. This stress no doubt left Martha mentally, physically and emotionally exhausted. In addition, she had a new baby, a girl named Nellie who was born in March 1864. In the middle of everything, Martha, trying to do the best she could with limited resources, was dealt the most heartbreaking loss a mother can endure, the death of a child. And then news came that Jacob was gone. Although government records report him as perishing in Salisbury Prison, North Carolina, Mattie claimed, "First, he was missing, then…he was being exchanged from Andersonville to Libby Prison, and he was near dead from starvation. They put him in what they called the hospital, and he died from the effects of starvation and was buried in a trench in the South. The neighbors took mother and us children to the old Fitch Schoolhouse and held a prayer over our dead father."

Martha could barely take a moment to mourn Jacob. She needed to provide for her children. She requested his pension and was denied, but she didn't back down, fighting to receive what was owed to her. She eventually succeeded in her quest after cutting through red tape and providing the requested documentation to prove she was Jacob's widow. At last, the government was satisfied and ruled her Jacob Dieter's legal widow, allowing her to not only receive his pension but also one hundred in back pay for his time spent in prison. Martha received eight dollars a month from Jacob's war pension and an additional two dollars a month for each child until they reached the age of sixteen. With this money, she bought a modest, comfortable home in Rochester and lived there until her death in 1904.

Mattie buried her mother in Oakwood Cemetery next to a large stone with her family name emblazoned across it. She was laid to rest at the foot of the stone in 1940, and her sister Nellie was buried there in 1952. Here, too, alongside Martha's grave, rises a marker with "Jacob" chiseled into the gray granite. It's a grave with no body, a remembrance for a beloved husband and father.

ANDREW CLARK MCCOY: MINNESOTA STATESMAN

In Jacob Dieter's letter from June 22, 1864, he mentions Andrew Cark "A.C." McCoy as a fellow prisoner, one of the men of Company F in the Ninth Minnesota Volunteer Infantry captured during the Battle of Guntown. McCoy, a Hamline University student and son of a Salem Township farmer immigrant from Illinois, spent seven months at Andersonville before being released in a prisoner exchange. After taking some time to recover from his ordeal, he returned to his company and fought in its Mobile Campaign in Alabama, which took place in the spring of 1865. The goal was to take Mobile, one of the Confederacy's largest cities and important commerce centers. It was believed that if the city fell, the Union would win the war. Notable battles during this campaign were the Battles at the Spanish Fort and Fort Blakeley. The campaign proved to be successful for the Union, and Mobile fell after two weeks of intense sieging.

Andersonville Prison, Andersonville, Georgia. *U.S. Library of Congress.*

After being discharged on August 22, 1865, McCoy returned to Rochester to farm with his father. He married Lydia Little on April 16, 1867, and pursued a career in civil service. Titles he held included town clerk for fifteen years, school board member for thirty years, town supervisor and county commissioner. He was also elected as a Republican state representative from 1903 to 1904 and again from 1907 to 1908, representing Olmsted County District Four. During his two terms as a representative, he participated on several committees, with focuses on agriculture, hospitals, logs and lumber and public buildings. His photograph in *The Legislative Manual State of Minnesota 1907* reveals a distinguished and handsome man with a gray and white–peppered moustache and beard, possessing a confident bearing and a straightforward stare.

A transcript of McCoy's speech about his experiences as a prisoner of war exists in the History Center of Olmsted County's archives. He mentions their arrival, "Oh! What a sight met our eyes as we entered the prison and the terrible stench that greeted our nostrils—men half naked— complexion colored by sun and pitch pine, smoke-haggard countenances, flesh shriveled and drawn tight to the bones, eyes sunken and glassy— it was difficult to believe that they belonged to the same race of beings as ourselves." And he described the horror of the filth and vermin population, "The little demons increased in number and size most rapidly and throve the best of anything I ever saw or heard in all of God's creation—I know they sapped the life's blood from many a poor fellow's veins....The ground was alive with the vermin. It was no unusual thing to have the outside of our clothes covered in the morning so thick that we could scrape off these pests with a knife, or rather a stick with the edges sharpened."

In a September 28, 1961 *Rochester Post-Bulletin* article, McCoy was reported to have described his experience of leaving Andersonville in a speech given at a family reunion a few years after the war's conclusion:

Andrew Clark McCoy. *From* The Minnesota Secretary of State's Legislative Manual, State of Minnesota, *1907.*

> *As fast as our names were written down, we were separated from the rest and were formed in a separate line. As soon as there was a trainload of us, we were marched to a vacant corner of the stockade, where we stayed that night under a special guard. The next morning, we went through the gate en route to the station three-quarters of a mile away, walked along the road between a file of guards. It took me a half day to walk that distance and I did my best.*
>
> *We boarded a flat car and rode all night in an awful cold rainstorm. Arriving at Savannah in the morning, we found men with tables and blank paroles for us to sign....After all the men had signed their paroles, we were marched to the river past Fort McCallister and to our fleet of transports.*

Close to 200 men from the Ninth Minnesota Volunteer Infantry Regiment were held as prisoners at Andersonville, and 123 perished within its stockade log walls. After his release, McCoy related how some prisoners in poor health were taken to hospitals, while the healthy men transported to Annapolis, Maryland, "had the joyous satisfaction of planting our feet once more in 'God's Country' and standing beneath Old Glory, free."

RHODA PIERCE GEORGE: AN OFFICER'S WIFE

During the Civil War, it was not unusual for the wives and children of soldiers, particularly those of officers, to spend time at army camps, just as Martha Dieter and her family had lived three months on Minnesota's frontier prairie at Fort Ridgley, earning small compensation for doing various jobs. Some infantry families journeyed farther from home, heading south and living close to small skirmishes and more intense battles. One such wife was Rhoda Pierce George, the spouse of Colonel James George of the Minnesota's Second Volunteer Infantry Regiment, Company C.

Colonel James George. *History Center of Olmsted County.*

Rhoda married James in 1842. They settled in Ohio, and their first child was born in 1844. Rhoda had experience being a soldier's wife, since James had served as the captain of an Ohio regiment during the Mexican-American War and had been injured in the Battle of Monterey in California on July 7, 1846. She and her husband were also among Olmsted County's pioneer settlers, moving in 1854 to Oronoco Township, where they bought a farm. They didn't farm for long, deciding instead to move a few miles southwest to Wasioja in Dodge County. The town was small but had much potential, and its population was predicted to grow tenfold within the next few years. Rhoda and James believed it was a good place to raise their young family. James practiced law out of a small square building among a respected seminary, several retail establishments, a productive flourmill along the Zumbro River and a prospering hotel near a well-traveled stagecoach line. A patriotic army man, George answered his country's call for more young men to enlist during the Civil War. Using his law office as a recruiting station, he asked for recruits. Eighty seminary students walked through the station's door, signing their names to a list of volunteers. These men made up 80 percent of the Second's Company C. On June 25, 1861, Rhoda and her children said goodbye to James as he left with his recruits, heading to Fort Snelling, Minnesota's military headquarters. Company C was mustered in on June 29, 1861, and James became lieutenant colonel. Company C headed to Fort Abercrombie for military training. The fort was located on the Red River along Minnesota's most Western edge, in what would become North Dakota. During their two-month stay, the United States–Dakota War began, and the fort was on alert for attack. On September 3, 1862, the fort experienced a six-hour

Dodge County Civil War recruiting station, Wasioja. *Amy Jo Hahn.*

siege by the Dakota. Company C returned to Fort Snelling and reunited with other regiment companies before embarking south on October 14. Among the regiment traveled Rhoda and her son, Ned.

While camped in Lebanon Junction, Kentucky, about thirty-five miles south of Louisville, and eventually stationed farther south in Lebanon, Kentucky, Rhoda cooked and cleaned for the soldiers, commented on how nice the people were and wrote many letters to her daughters and family, telling them how much she missed them. On January 1, 1862, James's regiment left Lebanon and marched farther south toward Campbellsville, leaving Rhoda and Ned behind. In a letter dated the day James left, Rhoda mentioned how lonely she felt, "If they stop in a place where I can follow with safety, I shall go very soon. If not, I will have to stay here, and if I do have to stay, I don't know what I shall do with Pa gone away off south to be shot at and my children away up in the frozen regions of the north where it would be almost impossible to get to them if I was to try. But I could not think of going home while Pa is in so much more danger than my children." Her attitude concerning Lebanon drastically changed after James's departure. She hated the cloudy and dreary weather without the sun or moon, and mentions in her letters she was unwell. In a January 11, 1862 letter addressed "Dear Girls at Home," she wrote sadly, "I don't know, but we have got to the place where darkness covers earth and gross darkness the people. The mud is awful here.…I don't believe I like old Kentucky as well as I did a short time ago." In the same letter she lamented:

> *Oh, Wretched War, where or when will it end? The general hospital is here now instead of Louisville. There is a tremendous big hall here, and that is taken for a hospital. I should think there are four or five hundred in it now, and the sick soldiers will be sent back here.…I am afraid I can't go away further with Pa. I sometimes have a notion to start home. It is so sickly here that I am awful afraid little Ned will get sick, but I feel as if I could not leave Pa until something is done.*

Under constant stress that she or Ned would catch the illness that was affecting the hospital patients, worried about the enemy drawing close and what she would do if they did and without the calming presence of her husband, Rhoda struggled to maintain her positivity. A January 15, 1862 letter to her "Dear Children" expresses her battle:

> *This is an awful lonesome, gloomy place. We have not seen the sun but twice, a few moments at a time, for the last fifteen days. I suppose you wonder I live at all. It is strange, I am surprised at myself, but I try not to look on the dark side. What awful calamity may befall us, we do not know. But one thing is, I would start home, but I can't leave Pa now, for he is surely in more danger than he has been at all. The sickness in this awful climate will kill more than all the shooting will.*

While Rhoda endured her misery, James and the Second Minnesota engaged in the first battle of their deployment on January 19; this battle also gained the status of being the Union's first major victory. It was called the Battle of Mill Springs and occurred near Nancy, Kentucky, in Wayne and Pulaski Counties. After receiving a promotion to colonel after the battle, James wrote to his children in Minnesota on January 30, "We had a hard time truly.…A hard, close fight and most terrible march pursuing the flying enemy over roads, the worst I ever saw, for eight miles. The mud deep enough to bury both men and horses and raining half the entire day and then at dark [arriving] just in front of the Rebel [line], we lay our men down on the wet ground without any protection whatever." His letter mentions he telegraphed Rhoda to join him at the new camp and that she and Ned would arrive soon.

By March 18, James was stationed near Nashville, Tennessee, and Rhoda and Ned were on their way home because it had become too dangerous for them to remain with the Confederate army threatening and the regiment heading to a new location. While Rhoda waited anxiously for word at home, James continued leading the Second Regiment in several military campaigns, including the Battle of Chickamauga, during which the Union suffered one of its biggest defeats. Its casualty number of 34,624 is second only to the Battle of Gettysburg. Despite the outcome, James bravely commanded his forces, and according to *History of Olmsted County, Minnesota* (Leonard, 33):

> *While the regiment was in a most exposed position, at a critical point in the line, General* [George Henry] *Thomas, the commander, in reconnoitering the line, wishing to assure himself of the reliability of the regiment in the emergency, rode up to Colonel George and asked, "Colonel, how long can you hold this position?" The colonel answered, "We will do the best we can, General." Again, General Thomas asked the same question and, receiving the same answer, said, "I must know, Colonel, can you hold the place?" To this, Colonel George answered, "General, if is your orders, you will find this regiment here at the expiration of their term of service." And they not only held the position but drove the enemy.*

After gaining much respect and admiration from his regiment and fellow officers throughout his Civil War tenure, James resigned on June 29, 1864, due to poor health. He was reunited with Rhoda and his children, and by 1870, the family was residing in Rochester, where James practiced law. James died on March 7, 1882, at the age of sixty-two, after experiencing heart problems. His death was noted in several newspapers, including the *Duluth Herald*, the *Alexandria Post*, the *New Ulm Weekly Review*, the *Western Minnesota Press*, the *Stillwater Messenger* and the *Saint Paul Daily Globe*. An undated and unnamed obituary located in the History Center of Olmsted County archives expresses gratitude for his "active and honorable service in two wars, his devotion to the honor and best interests of his country shone with distinguished splendor on the field of mortal strife, while all civil trusts committed to him have been discharged with singular fidelity and ability. Generous, large-hearted, social and endowed with rare conversational powers."

Rhoda died on August 25, 1896, after a long battle against breast cancer. Her obituary in the August 18, 1896 *Rochester Post* doesn't include a mention of the five months she spent encamped with her husband's regiment, but it does give insight to her strength of character and ability to endure the most traumatic of life's situations. "She has been suffering for the past eight years with cancer of the breast," reads the obituary. "Operation after operation has been performed, but only temporary relief has been afforded. For this past seven weeks, life has been at such a low ebb that her death was momentarily looked for."

William Henry Costley:
Illinois Twenty-Ninth Colored Infantry

Located on the old Rochester State Hospital grounds in what is now Quarry Hill Park, a popular hiking location on the city's northeast side, is a picturesque two-acre cemetery, the final resting place of 2,019 state hospital patients. For several decades, the cemetery went unnoticed, its small cement markers sinking into the ground or completely disappearing and its dead fading into Rochester history. But the dead have stories to tell—about who they were, why they were in Rochester and how they died. A group of people believed it was important to reveal these stories, to give voice to the people who had long been forgotten. They formed a nonprofit organization whose goal was to preserve the cemetery and identify and provide gravestones for each person buried in the grassy glen. One fascinating story discovered during the process rests with the man located in plot A6. Although the gravestone misspells his name as "Crossley," it has been verified that it marks the grave of William Henry Costley, the son of the first enslaved person freed by Abraham Lincoln.

Costley was the eldest son of Benjamin Costley and Nance Legins-Costley of Pekin, Tazewell County, Illinois. Nance was an indentured servant born into slavery in Kaskaskia, Illinois, to Randall and Anachy Legins. The July 1841 Illinois Supreme Court case *Bailey v. Cromwell* decided Nance and her children's fate. The estate of Dr. William Cromwell sued Major David Bailey, declaring he owed money for Nance. Bailey had entered into a transaction agreement with Cromwell for the purchase of Nance and signed a promissory note, agreeing to pay $400. However, Bailey agreed to pay only if presented with legal paperwork verifying Nance was a voluntary indentured servant. Under Illinois law, it was illegal to keep someone in indentured servitude if they didn't voluntarily give written consent. Bailey asked Abraham Lincoln to represent him, and the case made its way through the court system, leading Lincoln, just five years into his law career, to appear before the state's highest

Above: Rochester State Hospital Cemetery. *Amy Jo Hahn.*

Left: Abraham Lincoln, 1860. *U.S. Library of Congress, F. D'Avignon, John H. Bufford.*

court, defending his friend and Nance's right to be a free person. Since no legal papers could be found or presented, the Illinois Supreme Court handed a victory to Lincoln and Bailey, stating in its ruling, "It is a presumption of law, in the State of Illinois, that every person is free, without regard to color. The sale of a free person is illegal." Nance was a free woman, as were the infant William and his siblings.

At the age of twenty-five, Costley enlisted as a private in the Illinois Twenty-Ninth Colored Infantry on September 21, 1864, in Springfield, Illinois. As it is on his grave, his name is spelled incorrectly in his enlistment papers. He is listed as "Corsley." Misspelled names were not uncommon, especially when they were communicated by someone who was illiterate. A large "X" is located on the signature line, with his first and last names written in script on either side of it. An "X" mark on documentations indicates that the signee could not write.

On April 1, 1865, near the end of the war, Costley participated in the Battle of Five Forks in Dinwiddie County, near Petersburg, Virginia. Major General Philip Sheridan led the Union army, while Confederate major general George Pickett commanded the Army of Northern Virginia. It was vital for the Confederate army to maintain control of the South Side Railroad. Sheridan and his Union forces were victorious, and when the Battle of Five Forks concluded, one thousand Confederates were dead, another four thousand were taken prisoner and the South was dealt a devastating blow, with a major supply and evacuation route extinguished. During the battle, Costley was wounded. Author Carl Adams wrote in *Nance: Trials of the First Slave Freed by Abraham Lincoln* that an artillery shell exploded near Costley, its force causing him to fall and resulting in severe bruising of his left shoulder. The severe pain Costley experienced from this incident put him in a medical hospital.

When he rejoined his regiment, Costley traveled on a ship as part of a two-thousand-man deploy under the command of Major General Gordon Granger. The soldiers were to be stationed near the Mexico border. They made a stop in Galveston, Texas, where, on June 19, 1865, Granger shared the news with the city's residents that the Civil War was over, the South had been defeated and all enslaved people were free. It was the first time that enslaved people in Texas learned they were free. The historic day would become known as Juneteenth.

After being mustered out of the military on September 30, 1865, Costley returned to Illinois. By 1881, he was living in Iowa and was married to Mary Rebecca Webster; they had a daughter named Emma. Two years later,

William Costley's misspelled grave. *Amy Jo Hahn.*

he was divorced and married to Margaret Hartman. By 1886, Costley and
Margaret had also divorced, and Costley was residing in Minnesota. He was
admitted to the Rochester State Hospital with a diagnosis of dementia in
1888, dying on October 1 of that year.

3

Aviation

George Willard Furlow: World War I Flying Ace

During World War I, the distinction of being a "flying ace" was first awarded to military pilots who shot down five or more enemy planes during combat. The Great War's most famous ace was German pilot Manfred von Richthofen, who was given the nickname the "Red Baron." It was the first war to use aerial combat, and the creation of the "flying ace" title had more to do with a military public affairs strategy than military prowess, but it sounded impressive and romantic, and it was no small feat to target and bring down enemy planes while dodging hostile fire and maintaining flying altitude. The American people gobbled up the heroic stories of their young, daring, handsome men who defeated German enemies in the sky from the cockpit of an airplane, a relatively new invention that still mystified and entranced the general public. Rochester had its very own flying ace, Lieutenant George Willard Furlow.

Furlow was a member of the 103rd Aero Squadron, which was the first American pursuit squadron. By the end of its World War I service, the 103rd would claim the title of having the longest combat service of any squadron. Furlow's squadron flew the French fighter aircraft SPAD S.XIII. Furlow was credited with five air combat victories. He shared wins with other American pilots, a common occurrence because squadrons fought together against German fighters. His first victory with Edgar Tobin was

A 103rd Aero Squadron plane, World War I. *U.S. Air Force.*

recorded on August 11, 1918, in northeast France. On September 13, he found himself face to face with the enemy in the skies above Charey, France. His squadron was outnumbered—three planes to the Germans' seven. He, along with fellow squadron pilot Charles R. d'Olive, teamed up to bring down two of seven German planes, causing the others to retreat. For this heroic act, he was awarded the Distinguished Service Cross by the Air Service, United States Army. His fourth victory took place on September 17 above Verneville, France, where he once again found himself outnumbered by enemy aircraft. He was patrolling the airspace with two squadron members when a formation of eight German planes descended on them. Once again, his squadron was outnumbered, and once again, he didn't back down. In the vicious battle that ensued, Furlow's plane was damaged, and the outcome looked grim, but he didn't give up, putting up a defensive fight, which finally resulted in the destruction of one of the attacking planes. His stubborn refusal to quit, along with the relentless pursuit and skilled maneuvers of his teammates, forced the German fleet to retreat. For this outstanding feat, a bronze Oak Leaf Cluster was added to his medal ribbon. His fifth and final win, shared with two other pilots, occurred on October 27 in northeast France.

Rochester residents eagerly followed the valiant acts of their hometown "Bill" from the time of his enlistment in June 1917 to the day he returned home. The local papers ran articles starring the city's most popular son, and friends and family members gave permission for personal letters from him to be published. George wrote in June 1918:

> *We fly the smallest and fastest machines the allies make. They are very tricky, and one must watch them carefully....Our machines are equipped with a couple of machine guns, and they are synchronized to shoot through the propeller when turning. The only way one can aim is by aiming the machine. When two planes are combatting and going about 140 miles an hour, you can see that this requires considerable maneuvering. The better you can maneuver, the longer you will live, so I am practicing acrobatics every day. It looks kind of funny from the ground to see a machine flip flopping around in the air, but these stunts are useful when it comes to fighting, so why worry about the looks. I will be glad when I get on the front and get a chance to put these stunts into practical use.*

His courageous exploits also caught the attention of the entire state, with the *Minneapolis Morning Tribune* writing on December 6, 1918, about how his "extraordinary bravery in leading squadrons against superior enemy forces" led to his two honorable military citations. Of his military successes, Furlow wrote in a September 1918 letter about his first air combat win: "I now have credit for one plane that was brought down a few days ago but wasn't confirmed until today. The credit is split between another man and myself, as we attacked him together, both of us shooting at him, and it is difficult to determine which one of us really got him, so we both get credit....This is a wonderful game, and I like it more every day."

Even though he enjoyed flying, George decided not to pursue a career as a pilot in the commercial airlines industry after the war, stating in an interview that he was "satisfied with [his] airplane experience" and was "glad to be back in Old Rochester, the best place in the world, and in due time, [he thought he would] begin the study of law."

Although he was the most celebrated, George was not the only Furlow brother willing to sacrifice his life on the Western Front. Allen and Walter also served. Like George, Allen was a pilot. He flew several missions before being shot down, the resulting injuries preventing him from flying again. Allen earned a law degree from George Washington University and returned home to practice for a few years before being elected a Minnesota senator. He represented Minnesota's First District in the U.S. Congress for two terms, an integral player in the passage of legislation making all military pilots officers. In his appreciation, Charles Lindbergh sent Allen a warm thank-you. Allen was also a local newspaperman and retail investor. He lived in Washington, D.C., for a few years after leaving Congress, working as a lawyer for Curtiss-Wright Corporation and the Veterans Administration. After leaving Washington, D.C., Allen practiced law until he died in 1945. George attended Georgetown University and lived in Washington, D.C., for many years with a career in real estate. He died in 1959 from a heart condition at the age of sixty-six.

LOTTIE SCHERMERHORN: DARING WINGWALKER

On the morning of Tuesday, September 14, 1920, a large crowd gathered at the Olmsted County Fairgrounds to witness a teenager parachute from an airplane at a height of one thousand feet. Word had spread about the brave sixteen-year-old Lottie Schermerhorn after her August parachute

Lottie Schermerhorn and her pilot preparing for an aerial stunt performance. *History Center of Olmsted County.*

jump, which had earned her recognition as the first Minnesota woman to attempt such a feat, and hundreds flocked to get a glimpse of this aviatrix extraordinaire.

The spectators watched in awe as Lottie jumped from a speeding plane into the blue autumn sky. All seemed fine with her plummet until a strong south wind veered her off course, causing the crowd to gasp with fright as she catapulted haphazardly to the ground. Her small body bounced roughly across a nearby field for a half a mile before several fair workers managed to grab the white billowing silk of her army parachute and bring her to a stop. Young Lottie survived the scary landing with hardly a scratch, and it cemented her standing as the first Minnesota woman—and one of the first women in the country—to parachute from an airplane.

While young Lottie perfected her stunts at county fairs in Minnesota, Iowa and South Dakota, her counterpart Lillian Boyer captured national attention for her sensational aerial stunts, which included hanging by one hand or by her toes or teeth from a biplane. Lillian also stood on the plane's top wing with her feet secured in a strap while her pilot looped the airplane. Other nationally known airplane stuntwomen included pilots Katherine Stinson, the first woman to accomplish a loop; and Bessie Coleman, the first Black and Native woman to earn a pilot's license. Lottie and Lillian came of age during the Roaring Twenties, a decade that gave rise to an interest in aviation due to the popularity of barnstorming, a term used to describe traveling air exhibitions that visited small towns in rural areas across the country. During barnstorming events, pilots showcased their talents, doing various aerial tricks. Their plane of choice was a World War I Curtiss-JN biplane, nicknamed the "Jenny." While Lillian entertained thousands with her wingwalking, automobile-to-plane changes and parachute jumps, Rochester's aviation darling captivated the people of Minnesota, including the attendees of the 1922 Minnesota State Fair.

Charlotte "Lottie" Barrons was only sixteen years old when she married forty-seven-year-old George Schermerhorn, a former balloon ascensionist from Predmore, Minnesota, on July 3, 1920. She had large brown eyes and a slender oval face framed by dark hair, styled in a short modern bob with blunt, straight bangs. People who knew her described her as a wild child, independent with a preference for pants instead of dresses, "a daring and athletic girl, being a leader in many childish pranks and escapades." Due to her husband's aviation background and her own adventurous spirit, she soon took an interest in wingwalking and parachute jumping. In a preview article of her performance that was held on July 4, 1921, at the Olmsted

Lottie Schermerhorn parachuting to the ground. *History Center of Olmsted County.*

Nationally renowned wingwalker Lillian Boyer during a midair exhibition, 1922. *U.S. Library of Congress.*

County Fairgrounds in Rochester, the *Daily Bulletin* wrote that Lottie was "the most sensational figure," walking on the wings of an airplane, climbing from the top to bottom wings and parachuting off the biplane mid-flight.

While Lottie proved to be quite the entertainer, gaining a large fan base throughout the region, there was constant scrutiny and confusion in regard to the extreme age difference between her and her husband. In fact, the September 17, 1920 issue of the *Minneapolis Morning Tribune* ran a story about Lottie with a headline titled "Father Parachuted; Now His Daughter Leaps From Plane." The article states:

> *Lottie Schermerhorn, sixteen-year-old daughter of an Olmsted County inventive genius, thrilled visitors of the Olmsted County Fair by jumping headlong from a plane as it passed over the throng. Garbed in a mechanic's suit with an army parachute, Lottie made the leap when one thousand feet above the grandstand. The great white cloth bloomed perfectly after she had plunged twenty or thirty feet, and the landing was perfect. Years ago, the girl's father used to jump* [from hot air balloons] *with the aid of parachutes.*

Articles like this led many to believe Lottie was George's daughter, and there were others who wondered if the teen bride was forced to do the stunts for money. During a July 5, 1922 *Rochester Daily Bulletin* joint interview with Lottie, George Schermerhorn responded to the critics: "She's a daring little woman. She wanted to do this stunt business. Folks in Rochester, some of them think that I made her do it, and they were talking about putting a stop to it, they thought she was nothing but a little kid. Why, she was the one that wanted to do it. She ain't afraid of nothing, are you, Lottie?" Although Lottie responded with a bold, "Why, there ain't nothing to be afraid of," the writer indicated that this may not have been the case, describing the "girl-wife" as "grave and unsmiling, and yet, in spite of her gravity, she was absurdly childish looking." When the reporter asked Lottie if she wanted to do it, she repeated she wasn't afraid, stating that she loved wingwalking. But George chimed in, "You know, a woman can make twice as much money as a man in this business." More doubt was cast about Lottie's willingness for the aerial stunts when her mother was interviewed; she stated her daughter wasn't strong or brave and that she cried before every flight. Lottie's mother also mentioned her disapproval of the marriage; it was obvious she lacked affection for George Schermerhorn and believed he was exploiting her daughter.

Throughout Lottie's short career, which ended when she divorced George in 1924, she never gave any indication she was forced to perform. She continued to claim she enjoyed flying, especially while wingwalking and performing other aerial acrobatics, and the public loved to watch her perform. Reporters for the *Rochester Daily Post and Record* wrote a front-page feature story titled "Flying with Lottie" for the July 5, 1922 edition, describing Lottie and her jump in great detail:

> *Framed in the tightly drawn helmet, which hid a wealth of pretty dark hair, the face of the girl looked handsome and expressionless....She was as if the tidal wave of experiences that had rolled across her emerging womanhood had left as it ebbed only a bare reef across which blew cool, infuriate winds of avid recklessness. Yes, it was the face of a stoic, yet the face of a girl—the face of youth back of which joy, laughter and thrilling new impulses lay hidden, smothered....The little girl-wife seemed unconscious that the hour of her performance was at hand, her slender fingers locked tightly around her khaki-clad limbs, and she stared ahead, silent and grave. Then suddenly, she twisted her body back and glanced at the pilot. Her slumberous eyes, black against the peculiar pallor of her fair skin, appeared as though lit from within their swarthy depths by unextinguished fires smouldering within the dark well of some volcano crater. The pilot smiled and nodded, and the girl rose quickly and skillfully, and before we were aware of it, she was out on the wing of the plane, her slim, young body silhouetted clearly against the sky-line. Her hand rested lightly on the strap that was to jerk open the parachute on her back and she surveyed the ground below her with a professional eye....Lottie was lifted off the plane, dropped for some distance until the parachute opened full and the wind seized her, bearing her directly north and toward the city.*

During the interview following the drop, Lottie insisted she was not afraid or nervous. She complimented her pilot for his smooth flying skills and said:

> *The parachute opened almost instantly, and after the first rush downward, I got my breath enough to see that I was dropping back toward the city. It seemed a long drop, and I could not help but laugh to see the people below me in the adjoining field scatter for fear I would land on them. The swaying back and forth made me kind of dizzy, but I shut my eyes for a few seconds, and when I opened them, I was all right again. I knew everything was going to be all right, although the left side of*

the parachute, flapping a little, made me kind of nervous. After I had dropped about halfway, I began to enjoy it and hoped I wouldn't drop too quickly. The wind kept carrying me back towards town, and pretty soon, I saw that I was going to be safe from any danger of landing in the barbed wire fences....I pulled at the strap to let the fullness of the parachute out a little and, sip, I came down pell-mell before I had hardly time to get my breath. I landed right on the soft ground.

Local newspaper articles nicknamed her "Daring Lottie," called her "plunky" and "cool" and referred to her as the area's "Intrepid Girl Stunt Performer." Her thrilling performances lasted only four years. Her career as an aviatrix ended in April 1924, following her divorce from George Schermerhorn. By the end of that same month, she married Winfield L. Berkins, and stories about her wingwalking and parachute jumping exhibitions disappeared from the local newspapers. Not long after Lottie's departure from the scene, most barnstormer pilots and stunt performers stopped entertaining due to the passage of the Air Commerce Act of 1926, which created the aeronautics branch within the U.S. Department of Commerce, a predecessor to the Federal Aviation Agency. This government body was given the authority to pass airplane safety regulations, such as requiring licensed pilots, certifying aircraft and establishing and enforcing air traffic rules.

Berkins died of a heart attack in Chatfield, Minnesota, while preparing for a fishing trip in the fall of 1948, and Lottie married William Matheny five years later in Fillmore County. She was living in Portland, Multnomah County, Oregon, when she died on September 21, 1979, at the age of seventy-five, William preceding her in death twenty years before.

In her twilight years, did Lottie reflect fondly on her short time as a regional celebrity, known for successfully completing dangerous air tricks? No evidence of her perspective has been found, but perhaps some insight to her feelings can be gleamed from a *Rochester Daily Post and Record* interview: "It was all over so quickly that I was sorry, because it is great sport, and the people get a big thrill out of it. It is very wrong for them to get the impression that my husband wants me to do it. I like to do it myself, and I am not the least bit afraid."

THE FIRST ROCHESTER AIRPORTS

The Rochester International Airport is located a few miles south of Rochester on 2,400 acres. It originated as the Rochester Municipal Airport, opening in 1960, but it experienced a name change in 1995 due to an increase in arrivals of international travelers, mostly Mayo Clinic patients. Although it's the city's best-known and longest-serving airport, it was not the first or even the second airport in the city. For many Rochester historians, it may even be considered the city's fourth.

During the 1920s, air transportation became a popular topic of conversation for Rochester residents. For a time, planes landed on a dirt runway on what was known as Graham Field, part of the Olmsted County Fairgrounds. This was also the site of several aerial stunt exhibits. But this location proved to be insufficient, and a place for larger planes and more frequent takeoffs and landings was needed. Business owners and the Mayo Clinic were increasingly interested in establishing an official city airport and connecting the area to larger cities, such as Minneapolis and Chicago, which would expand its reach into larger U.S. metropolitan areas and their international counterparts. An airport boasting respected national airline service would be a boon to the area. An airport was essential to Rochester's

Rochester Airways. *History Center of Olmsted County.*

An aerial view of Rochester Airways. *History Center of Olmsted County.*

economic viability. The first foray into achieving this goal was an airport located on Rochester's southwest side.

In March 1928, Lester Fiegel, H.J. Postier, Dr. T.J. Moore and Arnie Steinke pooled their money to incorporate Rochester Airways for $15,000. They opened Rochester Airways, Rochester's first official airport. The airport was located on a rented 40-acre farm about a mile west of Saint Marys Hospital. A new hangar housed planes used for flying lessons. The airport's arrival was exciting, and its June 15 dedication was well attended, with guests attracted in part by the aerial dog fighting demonstrations by the U.S. Army Air Combat Force. As thrilling as the concept of a city airport was, it soon proved to be unsustainable; the operation and maintenance costs were too much. A devastating blow to the airport's future occurred when Jefferson Airways selected Graham Field for its passenger service, with its first scheduled trip from Minneapolis arriving on Friday, July 13, 1928. The *Post-Bulletin* reported "the first official trips of a giant air liner this morning created a situation comparable to that when the first railroad train came to Rochester many years ago. Curious spectators crowded the field to see the pioneer air passengers step from the plane." The southwest airport would close four months later. Meanwhile, Mayo Properties Association's Rochester Airport Company, led by Albert J. Lobb, had purchased 285 acres of land in the southeast quadrant of the city, not far from Graham Field, for $150,000, planning for the design and construction of a larger and more viable airport.

By November 1928, the Rochester Airport was opened, with its first passengers arriving and departing via Universal Airways, which added Rochester on its route from Minneapolis to Chicago. By May 1929, Northwest Airlines had taken over for Universal Airways, Yellow Cab Airlines had stopped on its way from Minneapolis to Kansas City and a flying school had begun giving lessons. A dedication of the airport was held in June 1929 in conjunction with the city's Diamond Jubilee celebration. Dr. Charles Horace Mayo commenced the celebration with a speech and at its conclusion was spectacular show of aerial stunts, of which the June 12, 1929 edition of the *Rochester Post-Bulletin* described as "a series of air exhibitions led by the formation flight of three army pursuit planes and the exhibition flight of Charles 'Speed' Holman of Minneapolis, executive of the Northwest Airways, whose series of loops, banks and tilted flying drew the eyes of thousands who lined the fence of the field and whose cars extended far around the airport."

The Rochester Airport grew quickly, adding a 132-by-84-foot hangar and notable airmail service. By the fall of 1940, the airport was expanded to 370 acres, had four paved 3,500-by-150-foot runways lined with floodlights, a passenger depot and Northwest Airlines, Mid-Continent Airlines and Universal Air Lines served the city with several daily flights.

Hangar at the Rochester Airport. *History Center of Olmsted County.*

Robert Hinckley, the assistant secretary of commerce, speaking at the 1940 Rochester Airport dedication. *History Center of Olmsted County.*

To celebrate this growth, the upgrades and technological advances, a special dedication ceremony was held to honor the airport's success and growth on August 4, 1940.

Thousands of people attended the dedication on that warm summer day, paying an admission fee of ten cents. Officials and their planes from Northwest Airlines, United Airlines and Mid-Continent Airlines attended, as did the mayors of Minneapolis and Saint Paul. Edith Graham Mayo, selected by the American Mothers' Committee of the Golden Rule Foundation as the "American Mother for 1940," christened a Northwest Airlines Douglas DC-3 named *City of Rochester*. Her son Dr. Charles W. Mayo christened the American Airline flagship *Minnesota*, which was one of the first transportation planes named after a state. U.S. assistant secretary of commerce Robert H. Hinckley was the event's main speaker, and Jacqueline "Jackie" Cochran, the first woman pilot to break the sound barrier and to use Mayo Clinic's aviation oxygen mask, also attended the dedication. Dorothy Bigelow Carney, an airport employee, remembered Cochran's arrival and also recalled an earlier exchange between Cochran

Left: Jacqueline "Jackie" Cochran. *U.S. Air Force.*

Below: Rochester Airport/Lobb Field aerial view. *History Center of Olmsted County.*

and a male airport employee in an undated narrative titled "Early Memories of Rochester's Old Airport" located in the History Center of Olmsted County's archives:

> *I saw her get out of her plane, a Stagger Wing Beechcraft, dressed as if for a garden party—I expected to see her in a flying suit. She was no stranger to Rochester, having flown in and out many times. One of the radio-room stories was about her. She came up to the radio and weather room, which was on the second story of the hangar, asking about weather. The man on duty commented that he had given it to her pilot some time earlier. She told him in no uncertain terms, "I am the pilot. He is my co-pilot."*

During World War II, the Rochester Airport contributed to war the efforts. An aeronautic school trained pilots, and it was a service stop the Women's Air Force Service Pilots (WASPs) who were making cross-country treks delivering equipment and supplies. Often delivering the planes, they flew to Alaska, where Russian pilots would take them to the war front. A weather bureau was established at the airport, and a federal control tower and army barracks for the Eleventh Ferrying Service Detachment-Ferrying Division-Air Transport Command were constructed there. The military transport group consisted of engineers, mechanics and other technicians, as well as a few guards and administrative personnel who provided service, repairs and tests for the aircraft flown by the WASPS. At the conclusion of the war, the Mayo Properties Association sold Rochester Airport to the City of Rochester for $1, and by the end of 1952, it experienced a name change to Lobb Field, honoring its principal founder and then recently retired president. A bronze plaque was placed at the airport; it read: "In tribute to the faith, wisdom and devotion of Albert J. Lobb, this airport is named Lobb Field by the mayor and common council of the City of Rochester." By 1955, Lobb Field had outgrown its space, and the hunt was on for a new airport location south of town. Land was purchased, and the new airport was built for $4 million, opening in September 1960. And with this new airport's rise, Lobb Field faded into history, dissolving slowly into a neighborhood called Meadow Park, taking with it an important piece of Rochester's aviation past.

U.S. Air Force Radar Base: Cold War Defense

In a *Rochester Post-Bulletin* article dated August 20, 1954, readers were notified of the construction of a military establishment in northeast Rochester near the intersection of Viola Road and Sixtieth Street Northeast. A photograph showed cement being poured for the barracks, with the caption text reading, "Work on the aircraft control and weather station northeast of Rochester is progressing…barracks, mess hall, weather building, tower, etc., will cost $300,000 and take four hundred construction days to complete, with some fifty men employed at the peak of the work. From seventy-five to one hundred air force men will staff at the station to be located on twenty-two acres of Carlton Penz Farm, six miles northeast of Rochester in Haverhill Township."

The Cold War had definitely hit home, as they were building an air defense base; the job of its equipment and men was to search the skies, locating and identifying Russian planes invading U.S. airspace and guiding fighter jets to the aircrafts' locations so that they could be intercepted and escorted out of U.S. territory. Brigadier General William A. Matheny, commander of the 31st Air Division in Saint Paul, was in charge of the Rochester station. The 31st Air Division was "charged with air defense of the Upper Midwest and command radar sites, fighter-interceptor bases and numerous ground observer corps posts in providing round-the-clock protection against a surprise enemy air attack over the country's northern approaches" (*Rochester Post-Bulletin*, March 17, 1955). The Rochester base was home to the 808th Aircraft Control and Warning Squadron, which reported to the 31st Air Division. It was equipped with AN/TPS-1D radar, created by Bell Labs and designated as a ground-control intercept (GCI) station. Captain Marvin J. Hess, a Minnesota native, was selected as Rochester's commanding officer, and the station comprised roughly seventy-six military personnel.

Brigadier General William A. Matheny. *U.S. Air Force.*

Why Rochester? Well, there was a concern that enemy aircraft could cross over from Canada into the United States, threatening large Midwest cities. Since Minnesota is one of the country's northernmost states and also shares a border with Canada, Rochester was deemed a worthy site for a base installation. It was not the only air defense

Bell Labs AN/TPS-1D Search Radar. *U.S. Air Force.*

base in Minnesota or the region. There were others, and Rochester was an integral link in a well-designed chain of several. The station was considered at the time to be part of the "Pine Tree Line," a defense radar network, which ran across the border of the United States and Canada.

The air force held an open house for curious residents on Armed Forces Day in May 1956 from 10:00 a.m. to 4:30 p.m., with tours given every fifteen minutes, informational lectures and radar, weather and military equipment on display. By the spring of 1957, news had spread that the radar base was closing, with the *Rochester Post-Bulletin* reporting on April 13 the "reason for discontinuing the base was ineffectiveness of the radar installation" so far south of the Canadian border. Improved radar surveillance equipment had been put in place at distant early warning (DEW) sites in northern Canada. A June 17, 1957 *Rochester Post-Bulletin* article confirmed the closure with an official statement made by Matheny: "Due to improvements in radar equipment, the surveillance area of the 808th AC and W Squadron can now be covered by adjacent sites. This will result in greater air defense capability in this area. Phasing out of the Rochester station makes it possible for the United States Air Force to utilize its service in other areas."

Hess shared that he and his team "were warmly accepted as members of the community and will always remember its hospitality." Hess no doubt had many good memories of his time in Rochester. During his short tenure, he married Plainview High School economics teacher Jerry Jacobs; their double ring ceremony made local newspaper headlines in June 1956. Several of his squadron members were groomsmen. The base closed on July 1, and by September 9, all of the enlisted men and equipment had vanished, leaving the base a ghost town. Olmsted County took ownership of the property in 2017.

4

ENTERTAINMENT

KNOWLTON'S WINDOW DISPLAYS AND EVENTS

Once upon a time, locally owned department stores accented corners of cities across the country. These retail establishments offered more than simply a place to buy the latest clothing styles, hosiery, hats or shoes, they became social gathering places, offering a variety of events and often rotating window displays, reflecting the current holiday or newest arrivals. The stores became a source of entertainment for locals, and they flourished for several decades before the arrival of malls and buyouts from large chain stores. Rochester was no exception. Among its earliest and longest-lasting stores were the Massey & Co. and Knowlton's Department Stores.

Knowlton's had its origins in 1858, when John Blake opened his dry goods and merchandising business on Broadway Avenue. He named it J.D. Blake & Co. It became Blake & Leet for a time after A.D. Leet bought a controlling interest. After Blake left for Minneapolis, it was known as Leet & Knowlton, followed by E.A. Knowlton Co. before becoming Knowlton's Department Store. The owner most associated with its history is Elliott Ainsworth Knowlton. Knowlton worked at J.D. Blake & Co. as a young man. Through his employment, he met Ella Blake, J.D.'s sister. The two quickly fell in love and married. He eventually became the sole owner of the retail establishment after partnering for a few years with Leet. After Leet retired, Knowlton became the sole owner, giving the business his name. His sons, George and Clarence, continued running the business, buying it from their father in 1910, when his health began to fail. E.A. continued to be involved

Knowlton's Department Store. *History Center of Olmsted County.*

with the store until he died in 1927. George died four years later, leaving Clarence as the owner alongside his wife, Daisy, and daughter, Evelyn. The store remained in the family's hands, with an employee share purchase program started in 1945. It was later sold to Dayton's in 1952. Dayton's would construct a new six-story building in its place, and would remain on Broadway Avenue until moving to Apache Mall in 1972.

But before its demise, Knowlton's was one of Rochester's most popular shopping destinations, and it was the city's largest retail store during the 1930s and 1940s. It was famous for its impressive line of exterior windows, offering onlookers a glimpse at what was available for purchase inside. The themed window décor often made a splash with the local newspapers, enticing people to journey downtown to catch a look at the newest display. When it was announced that the store was expanding into larger quarters, straddling Zumbro Street and Broadway Avenue, the April 11, 1913 *Post and Record* reported, the street fronts "will give a splendid opportunity for the display of goods and will present a most imposing appearance. On both streets, the entrance will be constructed on the arcade plan, there being one door on Zumbro Street and two doors on Broadway, with mammoth show windows and plate-glass cases in the front of the arcade. Modern lighting and equipment will add to the attractiveness of this place."

Through its existence, Knowlton's hosted car shows, fashion shows, live animal exhibits, Santa visits, exclusive galas and customer appreciation events. One of its most popular events was the summer Peony Show and Parade. The inaugural show was held on Wednesday, June 23, 1927. According to a full-page advertisement placed in the local paper, flower submissions were "three blossoms of a kind displayed in milk bottle." Judging commenced at 2:00 p.m., with an auction following. The proceeds from the auction went to help fund the Olmsted County Fair. Outside, children participated in the colorful Peony Parade. The children's parade began at the Lawler Theatre and ended at Knowlton's, where prizes were awarded. The store's newspaper advertisement declared that one girl would win a prize for "best all-peony float with doll or baby buggy base" and one boy for "best all-peony float with coaster, wagon base." The show and parade were a hit—hundreds of customers flocked downtown to attend.

A car display inside Knowlton's Department Store. *History Center of Olmsted County.*

Knowlton's Peony Flower Parade of 1927. *History Center of Olmsted County.*

Knowlton's kept its loyal customers entertained and engaged through its various events and activities. It also invested time and money into creating arresting window displays—so much so that the Knowlton family employed a team dedicated to making the windows a success. On April 16, 1923, the *Rochester Daily Post and Record* ran an article about the store's display manager N.K. Markle and how the Knowlton's windows had earned an impressive national reputation. They were even featured in a national publication named the *Northwest Commercial Bulletin.* The store was featured on the publication's cover with a headline reading, "Windows Help make National Silk Week Success for Minnesota Firm." The first page "carries a beautiful photograph of a window in the E.A. Knowlton Store designed and arranged by Mr. Markle. With a clever array of spots and overhead lights, the local man has proven himself a real artist and the photograph is striking in every detail. It shows the latest styles in silk goods and is so arranged as to bring out the brilliant colors." The newspaper reprinted the *Northwest Commercial Bulletin*'s praise:

This prominent Southern Minnesota Department Store has splendid window display facilities, and these were utilized effectively during the week as the accompanying reproduction of one of the series of silk displays reveals most conclusively. The Knowlton display windows are one of the attractions of this Minnesota city, and realizing the advertising value inherent therein and their ability to arouse buying interest and transform passerby into purchasers, N.K. Markle, display manager, sees to it that they are at all times conveying the message of new and desirable merchandise attractively priced.

In December 1923, Knowlton's was among several retailers to produce festive holiday displays. "Stores that make a specialty of Christmas toys have attractive displays of the trinkets that please young folks. A fairyland of toys is shown in several windows, and the little tots revel in pressing their noses to the windows and in picking out the things they wish Santa would bring them," wrote the *Rochester Daily Post and Record* in its December 8 edition. "Santa himself makes his appearance every afternoon in the toy

An exquisite window display at Knowlton's Department Store. *History Center of Olmsted County.*

window at the E.A. Knowlton Company Store and points out some of the things he is going to bring around to this little friends later." Knowlton's Christmas window tradition dated to 1895, when the December 20 *Rochester Post* commented, "Leet & Knowlton have Santa Claus driving a spirited team of reindeer through a snow-covered avenue of stately pines. Their other windows contain articles best described as useful presents, to which they are calling special attention." Even though Knowlton's boasted impressive holiday adornments showcasing its merchandise, it was not the only downtown store to use windows to entice shoppers through the front door. The same article noted, "Trimming for Christmas trees appear in profusion at the window of the Queen City Tea and Coffee Company. They glisten very prettily under the electric lights," and "Stevens & Co. have a pyramid of dolls…a toy train winds its tortuous route along the base of the pyramid." Five years later, in its December 23 issue, the *Rochester Post* called the Christmas scene in the window of Massey & Co. "one of the most beautiful and artistic window displays it has been our pleasure to notice.…A Christmas tree made of fine linen in purest white; a large mirror reflects the snowy whiteness…a golden harp, whose music is that of unseen fairy hands…the background is a grating of white and red ribbons." For several decades, the downtown retail community went all out to attract holiday shoppers, lighting up the cold evenings between Thanksgiving and Christmas along Broadway Avenue and its side streets with warm lights and joyful creations.

It must have been a bittersweet moment for the entire community when it was announced that Knowlton's would close and sell to Dayton's, a Minneapolis-based department store company. At least Dayton's was somewhat local, and Rochester would be its first branch outside of the Twin Cities, a start to its growth as a regional chain store and eventual transition into the modern mammoth Target. However, a Rochester landmark and tradition vanished, its impressive brick-and-mortar building gone; its beautiful and unique window displays now legends. The *Post and Record* wrote in its April 11, 1913 issue, "The E.A. Knowlton Co. is one of the pioneer institutions of this city, and during the entire period of existence, it has been favored with an excellent patronage because of its high standards and business management. It is doubtful if there is a store better known to the people of southern Minnesota."

THE CIRCUS AND MUSIC MAN
WILLIAM "BILLY" FRIEDELL

In its earliest days, Rochester was considered part of the frontier, the expansive American West, since it was located west of the Mississippi and founded during Minnesota's territorial days. Since Rochester was located miles away from big city entertainment venues, traveling circus troupes filled this void, and residents welcomed them with enthusiasm. Names like Ringling Bros. and Barnum and Bailey, which eventually merged into "The Greatest Show on Earth," were among the most famous circus companies that toured across the U.S. and stopped in Rochester, but there were hundreds of others that traveled and performed across the country before their rise.

One of the first recorded circus troupes to visit Rochester came on August 8, 1860. The *Rochester City News* issues from July 25 and July 31 ran advertisements for Cooke's Royal Circus, heralding that the "unequaled European troupe, comprising all the great talent in the equestrian profession, will exhibit their splendid, novel and exciting feats of horsemanship and athletic skill." The August 4 *Rochester City Post* made a mention of the troupe's impending arrival, "Everybody and his wife and children are on the qui vive for the advent of Cooke's Royal Circus, whose magnificent handbills promise wonderful performances on the afternoon and evening of Wednesday next. Of course, everybody will go." The acts focused mostly on equestrian tricks but also included a contortionist, a leopard and acrobat demonstrations. Admission prices were fifty cents for adults and twenty-five cents for children. The following year, the R. Sands Combination Circus visited with another show filled with clowns, a live band and acrobatic and equestrian feats, including the "Gigantic Cavalcade," led by the "War Chariot of Achilles" pulled by a team of Arabian horses. On August 15, Castello and Van Vlick's Circus held two shows, and over one thousand spectators attended. The following day's *Rochester City Post* wrote, "The performance and music was equal to the best, and the trained horses excelled anything of the kind we ever saw." Throughout the 1860s, other circus groups making stops in Rochester included Old Cary's Circus, Orton Brothers Great American Circus, the Great Consolidation Circus, the Imperial Circus and Caldwell's Occidental Circus. Gorgeous horses and skilled equestrian riders and many beautiful women dressed in glittering costumes who wowed audiences with astounding feats were the main attractions of these early circuses.

But on Thursday, July 16, 1868, a new attraction took center stage when Bailey and Co.'s Great Quadruple Combination stopped in town, bringing

Circus tents erected along railroad tracks. *History Center of Olmsted County.*

with it an impressive menagerie of exotic animals in addition to its horse and human actors. The *Federal Union* wrote in its July 11, 1868 edition, "The citizens of this vicinity will have an opportunity…of indulging their curiosity and taste for amusement by visiting this splendid show and menagerie combined. The collection of animals is said to be the largest now in the West, and it comprises several rare specimens not usually met with in travelling caravans." The *Rochester Post* wrote on the same day, "The animal wonders exhibits are alone worth the price of admission" and "form an instructive show to which every parent should take his children." An accompanying advertisement listed the unique animals on display, such as a rhinoceros, a Tibetan yak, a polar bear, llamas, a lioness and her cubs, tigers, hyenas, jaguars, panthers, wolves, emus, bears, zebras, monkeys and a variety of exotic birds. In addition, there were Egyptian camels and African elephants, which were harnessed to a large chariot carrying the Withers Washington Cornet Band through downtown. The first description of a circus cavalcade parading along city streets appeared on July 10, 1861, when the *Rochester City Post* wrote about G.W. DeHaven's Union Circus showcasing a "grand procession" with the Great Union Bugle Band playing "the choicest strains of delicious harmony…with a splendid band chariot, drawn by superb steeds." However, witnessing such exotic animals marching through downtown was a new experience for Rochester and would become a highly anticipated tradition. When the circus arrived by train, people gathered downtown, lining the streets, eagerly waiting to see the diverse spectacle of animals. The first mention of a circus arriving by rail appeared in July 1875, when the *Rochester Post* ran a large two-column advertisement announcing the arrival on July 19 of Howe's Great London Circus. The circus consisted of forty-two rail cars, which included ten horse cars and two elephant cars, both measuring thirty-six feet in length.

Circuses would provide popular entertainment, with regular performances throughout the next several decades. Wrote Les Standiford in his June 15, 2021 online *TIME* article, adapted from his 2021 *Battle for the Big Top*:

> *For the better part of the century—a period that encompassed the Civil War, America's Gilded Age, World War I, and the Great Depression—the circus reigned as far and away America's premier form of popular entertainment. At the industry's peak, the day the circus came to town ranked with Thanksgiving, Christmas and the Fourth of July: banks and businesses closed, schools were dismissed, and an entire populace assembled on early morning main streets to watch the elephants and clowns and bejeweled entertainers parade from the train station to the circus grounds, where the big top was raised to house thousands for afternoon and evening performances.*

But it couldn't last. The industry eventually experienced a decline in interest and support, and dozens of traveling circuses folded one by one. The mighty Ringling Bros. and Barnum & Bailey's held on, lasting longer than others, but even "The Greatest Show on Earth" couldn't survive, the lights going dark for its big top forever in 2017.

It was the circus that brought musician William "Billy" Friedell to Rochester. Friedell became a respected businessman and influential member of the city's hospitality industry. But before arriving in the 1890s, he traveled with the Ringling Bros. circus, playing clarinet. After being with the circus for five years, he suffered a traumatic eye injury when a windstorm ripped through the big top tent, causing it to collapse. He traveled to the Mayo Clinic for treatment. After spending time in the city while undergoing eye removal surgery and glass eye placement, he decided to stay. During his first few weeks as a resident, he played a harp on Rochester street corners, asking appreciative spectators to leave some change. Billy's harp was a special heirloom, gifted to him from his father, a celebrated violinmaker at the Wurlitzer Music Company in Cincinnati, Ohio. He worked for a time

A circus parade through downtown Rochester, circa 1949–50. *History Center of Olmsted County.*

at the Rochester State Hospital, organizing an orchestra, which included hospital employees and patients. With high demand for professional music at area dances, parties and other events, Billy created yet another orchestra. He became a founder, bandleader and member of many different musical groups, including the Queen City Orchestra, Friedell-Cook Orchestra and Hausner's Orchestra. His orchestras were sometimes contracted with Mississippi and Missouri riverboats. He recalled his riverboat days in an interview for the February 14, 1960 *Minneapolis Sunday Tribune*:

> *Those were some boats. They had gambling and bartenders and all kinds of things. The boats were licensed to carry 1,500 people or three times that amount in freight because freight would lay still, but people would always move around if a town was on one side of the boat. We played on an excursion steamer, the* Jacob Richtman. *She was a beautiful thing. Painted red at the water's edge, then white in the center, and sky blue for the stack. She was like a ball of fire at night, steaming down the dark river.*

Billy Friedell with his heirloom harp, Hausner's Orchestra. *History Center of Olmsted County.*

He eventually owned the West Hotel and Florence Hotel and built and operated the Beverly Apartments, which offered housing for single women working as nurses, teachers and retailers. His daughters, Florence and Lauretta, were also musicians. Florence specialized in violin, and Lauretta in piano. Both played in the Lawler and Chateau Theatre Orchestras, providing soundtracks to silent films. At times, starting as small children, they were members of their father's various orchestras.

Billy died in 1969 at the age of ninety-six, a resident of Beverly Apartments, his daughter Florence living across the hall, often entertaining him with her music. Billy loved his life and never regretted settling in the Med City. "That was the best windstorm that ever happened," he recalled in the 1960 *Tribune* interview. "I'm happy that the circus tornado blew me into the best town anywhere. Rochester."

HORSE RACING AND THE EASTON FAMILY

As the famous bay harness racer Dan Patch cruised around tracks, scoring impressive times at record-breaking speeds, Rochester built its own respected racing community. Harness racing, consisting of trotters and pacers pulling a two-wheel sulky cart with a jockey at the reins, was extremely popular at the end of the nineteenth century and beginning of the twentieth century across the United States, and several of the city's most prominent individuals bred and raced horses, many boasting their own tracks and constructing large barns to house winning stock.

Some of the town's most colorful horse owners were the Eastons: James, Lucy and their son, Hamlet. James was a photographer by trade with a studio at 213 South Broadway Avenue, but he was also a farmer and owner of several successful racehorses. In addition to being listed in the city's business directory as a photographer, he was listed separately as a "breeder of fast horses." Lucy was a respected clairvoyant and magnetic healer, often addressed as Dr. Easton and listed often among medical physicians. According to Nora Guthrey in *Medicine and Its Practitioners in Olmsted County Prior to 1900*, several local physicians advised their patients to see Dr. Easton—not for help with physical ailments but to improve physiologic health. Lucy didn't just use her spiritual skills to help heal her human patients; she extended their use to include her family's barn of horses. A *Record and Union* March 7, 1890 article wrote, "[Lucy] used to go to the race track to talk with horses and cast a success spell on them." Lucy possessed an incredibly charismatic personality. She was a unique individual who easily attracted people to her specialized type of care. Guthrey described her as an interesting character, handsome and statuesque, sincere in her practice possessing a kind nature. She was an intelligent woman and an inventor; her 1890 patented flaxseed separating machine was mentioned in an article about Minnesota women inventors in the November 1, 1992 *Pioneer Press*.

Hamlet, known as "Hammy" or "Ham" but whose official moniker was James Hamlet Bolt Easton, was an avid racer, often in the sulky driver's seat and claiming top prize with his favorite equine, a black pacer called Badge E., whom he had raised since birth. His mother took a special interest in this beloved horse, and the August 14, 1896 *Rochester Post* reported, "[Lucy] holds a séance every forenoon of the day that Badge is to start a race. If the spirits tell her that Badge will win that day, the message is told by wire to the son, who governs his pool tickets accordingly." In addition to having a natural talent with horses, Hamlet was also an accomplished musician. The local newspapers ran story after story about his exquisite baritone voice. Rochester attorney Bunn T. Willson once discussed his friend's enthralling performances for a biographical sketch about the Easton family: "When some prominent guest was in Rochester, a reception and musicale would be given. Hamlet was there in his dress suit and white tie….when he stood near the piano and the rich, melodious notes fairly poured from his throat, they

Left: Hamlet Easton, a jockey and baritone extraordinaire. *History Center of Olmsted County, J.H. & L.J.B Easton Photo-Artists, (Rochester, MN)*.

Right: Dr. Lucy Easton, a clairvoyant and magnetic healer. *History Center of Olmsted County, Easton's Photographic Gallery (Rochester, MN)*.

realized they were receiving a real treat....He sang effortlessly—the notes rolling out with ease in an extremely wide range of tone; his notes were firm and sure, and tone shading was beautiful."

Hamlet pursued legal studies at Harvard Law School; however, he never pursued the profession, deciding instead to focus his energies on what he loved: music and horses. Hamlet became an integral part of the Easton racing business, and his beloved Badge gained national notice when he broke a world record with Hamlet as jockey. The October 12, 1894 *Record and Union* stated, "Badge has the best record of any Rochester horse that has been campaigned this season from the standpoint of both time and money." Badge was considered among the fastest pacers in the country during the height of his racing. He was of prestigious stock, being able to trace his lineage through both his dam and sire to Hambletonian, the Standardbred's foundation sire. He and another notable Rochester horse, Maud Wright, also a bay, shared a sire, Silas Wright, a grandsire of their dam, Allie Gaines, and most likely shared the same dam, Fanny Newton, a Morgan progeny owned by Rochester's C.M. Clough. Silas Wright, also owned by Clough, was a well-known local racer and was the majority winner of a much-anticipated annual race against M.T. Grattan's Herod. The two bay equine siblings often traveled to races together. Both were remarkable racers that gained loyal followers and fans. Maud Wright's success on the track garnered her national and international notice. She was eventually sold to Leopold Hauser of Vienna, Austria, and competed on the European circuit before being relegated to broodmare status in Hauser's stables. Her last colt, Lord Revelstoke I, was born in 1912. Although what happened to Maud Wright in her last years is not known, Badge remained with the Easton family until his death. Despite multiple offers for their star horse, the family refused to sell. He was considered part of the family. A few years after James died, Hamlet and his mother relocated to the Sunshine State, ending their racing endeavors. Both died there, Lucy in 1916 and Hamlet in 1921; they are buried side by side at Fern Hill Memorial Gardens and Mausoleum in Stuart, Florida.

Badge and Maud Wright were just two of the notable horses that put Rochester's name on the racing map. Another famous local horse whose racing prime dated to the 1870s was a black stallion named Star of the West. Star of the West raced all over the state and region but most often on tracks around the Twin Cities. The pretty and spirited ebony horse proved to have a long career, exhibiting amazing stamina, and was still racing at the age of twenty-two. A huge audience turned out in 1881 to witness one of his last races at the Minnesota State Fair, which was held in Rochester. The *Rochester Post* wrote about the black horse's surprising and welcome victory in its September 16, 1881 issue:

> *That the victory of the old horse was especially satisfactory to the large crowd in attendance was evidenced by the thunders of applause which followed men, women, and children rising to their feet in their excitement and cheering, clapping their hands, waving handkerchiefs and in every way possible expressing their satisfaction at the result and admiration for the gallant old horse. After verifying the weights, the harness was removed from the veteran, and he was led in front of the judges' stand, where a wreath, the work of deft hands of several of Rochester's fairest daughters was placed upon his head.*

The impressive pedigrees and racing skills of the colts and fillies produced in Rochester and the racing enthusiasm that supported local tracks, including

Harness racing, Olmsted County Fairgrounds. *History Center of Olmsted County.*

a favorite at the Olmsted County Fairgrounds, made the city a hot spot for the industry west of the Mississippi River. In the city's earliest days, a half-mile dirt track located where Soldiers Field now sits attracted racers from all over the country. From spring to fall, the city vibrated with horse fever, and racing results were covered widely in the local newspapers. Attending the races was an afternoon affair, and people dressed in their very best attire, with gentlemen in suits and ladies in fancy hats. By 1910, the city's racing heyday was over, but there was still interest in the sport and a call to not abandon it. The *Post and Record* wrote on September 7, 1906:

> *Rochester is not dead yet as a racing center. A little of its pristine glory still hangs over it like a mist through which dim shapes and shadows take form and a phantom hand writes records of races which once were the pride of not only Olmsted County and Southern Minnesota, but the whole northwest. Time cannot efface the memories of the fast events which were pulled off on the old racecourse, nor shut out the raucous cheers of the crowd in the grandstand as a favorite came down the stretch and under the wire at the judges' stand.*

Racing never came back into the popularity it had once enjoyed, but it didn't completely vanish. For the next several decades, harness racing continued in a much smaller capacity, with heats sometimes held at the Olmsted County Fairgrounds Racetrack.

SHIRLEY HAR: SHIRLEY O'HARA, MOVIE STAR

During the 1930s and 1940s, young women across the country left their homes to journey to Hollywood. They carried with them dreams of fame and fortune, imagining evolving into the next Marlene Dietrich or Rita Hayworth. But for many of these fresh-faced hopefuls, nothing similar to their dreams ever materialized. Some were asked to sign four- to seven-year film studio contracts, but that didn't guarantee starring film roles or even speaking parts. Many became studio-owned starlets, working at the mercy of powerful studio executives. They were usually given minor roles, seldom with speaking lines, and they were often used as beautiful extras in the backgrounds of shots. While many struggled to claim their film careers and others gave up and moved back home, Rochester native Shirley Har sort of stumbled into a career in the movies.

Being a movie star was the furthest thing from Har's mind while growing up. Her family recalled in a June 5, 1943 *Rochester Post-Bulletin* article how she'd never been interested in a career on screen and that her "stage ambitions began and ended with dancing lessons from the time she was eight years old until she had passed her twelfth birthday." Har was determined to pursue a career as a crime reporter after graduating from high school. She was so interested in this line of work that as a teenager, she approached the *Rochester Post-Bulletin* for a job writing crime stories. The paper turned her down. She was disappointed but was soon offered a job at the Chateau Theatre. "I was the drawing girl for bank nights," she recalled in a June 2, 1980 *Rochester Post-Bulletin* interview. "I was assigned to draw the winning tickets. The pay wasn't great [fifty cents a week], but I did get to see every movie that came along for free." This, her first peak at the film industry, perhaps piqued her interest in an eventual Hollywood career. According to her family, although she never participated in a high school play, she was a movie enthusiast.

When Har graduated from Rochester High School in 1942, the words "'Princess' ought to be able to get plenty of famous peoples' autographs when she is a crime reporter" were written under a glamorous senior yearbook portrait. It was obvious her peers regarded her as beautiful, smart and ambitious. The summer after graduation, she traveled to Utah and California, staying with friends along the way. When she arrived in Hollywood, she decided to stay because she liked the area. She quickly secured a job as an elevator girl at the Saks Fifth Avenue store in Beverly Hills. With a charming smile, an immaculate uniform draping her 118-pound, five-foot-four-and-half-inch-tall frame and a bouncy new

Shirley O'Hara on the front page of *Know Rochester*, February 1944. *History Center of Olmsted County.*

hair cut, she transported Saks customers from floor to floor with style. In a letter sent to her mother, Har wrote enthusiastically about how her hair garnered much attention, receiving "compliments galore from all the actresses she piloted up and down the elite store." Her popularity at Saks helped advance her from operating the elevator to the hosiery counter. Then her big break came.

In flowing script in a 1943 letter written on letterhead from the Hollywood Studio Club, a famous residence for single young women pursuing movie careers, to Miss Aletha M. Herwig, a Rochester High School teacher, Har shared she had three job advancements at the store within seven months, stating proudly: "I was the youngest saleslady in the store. I soon had a very good clientele. One of my good customers was a big producer's wife. She mentioned me to the talent scout for RKO at a dinner one night, and the next day, his secretary called me at Saks and asked me if I could come out as soon as possible, for Mr. Ruben would like to see me. To make a long story short, I was the type they were looking for, am now under contract and started my first picture last Monday."

Har went on to mention she had a beautiful wardrobe on set and that her role involved seven costume changes. She also lamented a bit about changing her name from "Har" to "O'Hara." The changing of a name was a common occurrence within the studio system. She worried no one in Rochester would recognize the new name and that the *Rochester Post-Bulletin* wouldn't know it was her when the movie publicity materials arrived in the newsroom.

O'Hara's first two RKO films, *Gildersleeve on Broadway* and *Government Girl* were headlined by famous film stars Billie Burke ("Glinda" from *The Wizard of Oz*) and Olivia de Havilland ("Melanie Wilkes" from *Gone With the Wind*). After a third turn in *Around the World*, O'Hara landed a rather unique role in a psychological thriller titled *The Ghost Ship*, giving her a first taste of fame. For the film, RKO publicized a competition among its contracted actresses for the role dubbed "Shadow Girl." The character would appear at the end of the horror film and only as a silhouette projected on the side of a ship amid fog and shadows. So intriguing was this unusual competition that *LIFE* magazine showcased the search in its September 13, 1943 issue. The article highlighted several actresses who auditioned for the part, including eventual Emmy winner Barbara Hale and Oscar winner Dorothy Malone. The actresses were shown in side-by-side comparisons, with their studio publicity photographs alongside their silhouette images. *LIFE* wrote, "To find the shapeliest "shadow girl," the studio (RKO) dressed these girls in skin-tight bathing suits and had them parade behind a screen. Resultant silhouettes looked like everything from glamorous radiator caps to French postcards. The winner of this contest in curvilinear design was eighteen-year-old Shirley O'Hara."

RKO continued to cast O'Hara in unaccredited bit parts, but the 1944 *Seven Days Ashore* garnered her more attention, her curly brown hair attracting the notice of movie audiences. Fans began asking their hair stylists to copy O'Hara's unique cut. Her bouncy bob was styled by Hazel Rogers, RKO's head hairdresser whose talent had been on Oscar-winning display in MGM's 1939 best picture winner *Gone with the Wind*. So popular was the cut that it was described in several women's magazine advertisements as a "youthful easy-to-fix hairdo....Short, brushed up around the head to form an aura, the front is marked by soft bangs. A short-left part breaks the smooth crown in the 'O'Hara bob.' The hair is brushed up all around."

O'Hara's first credited role came shortly after the release of the "O'Hara Bob" when she was awarded the part of Athena, an Amazon princess, in the 1944 RKO film *Tarzan and the Amazons*. Johnny Weissmuller starred as the titular character for the ninth time, with Brenda Joyce appearing for the first time as Jane Parker, taking over the character for Maureen O'Sullivan, who appeared in six previous Tarzan features when they had been distributed by MGM. O'Hara often credited *Tarzan and the Amazons* as "her most important picture" and one of her favorites.

When not busy making movies for RKO, O'Hara joined many aspiring actors and those of the more famous variety volunteering for the war effort at the Hollywood Canteen. It was located at 1451 Cahuenga Boulevard in Hollywood and operated from October 3, 1942, to November 22, 1945. The Hollywood Canteen offered free entertainment and hot meals for U.S. servicemen. Actors Bette Davis, John Garfield and Jules Stein, a popular talent agent and founder of the Music Corporation of America (MCA), founded the popular hangout. From its opening to its closing, over three thousand film industry professionals donated their time and money to its success. As part of her volunteer work, O'Hara waited tables, cooked in the kitchen, cleaned tables and danced with soldiers. For her wartime volunteer work, O'Hara received the Support for America Award.

O'Hara married Jimmy McHugh Jr. and had a son, Jimmy McHugh III. They lived in England for a few years when McHugh took a position as head of the MCA London office. MCA was a powerful player in the entertainment industry. It began as a talent agency for musicians but quickly expanded into the film, television and publishing industries; it is the predecessor of

NBCUniversal. O'Hara's second marriage was to Milton Krims, an actor, screenwriter, novelist and journalist.

After her foray into films, O'Hara enjoyed a long acting career on television, guest starring in hits such as *The Mary Tyler Moore Show*, *The Twilight Zone*, *The Bob Newhart Show*, *Marcus Welby, MD* and *Gunsmoke*. Her last movie role was as Mrs. Kramer in 1980's *Getting Wasted*. For a time, she owned Publicity West, a publicity firm that promoted Warner Bros. and Columbia Pictures. She also worked as publicity director for Warner Bros. before retiring from the business. On December 13, 2002, O'Hara died at the age of seventy-eight from diabetes complications in Calabasas, California. Even though she didn't become as famous as Betty Grable or Joan Fontaine, she was a product of the golden age of Hollywood, working behind and in front of the camera. Perhaps the *Rochester Post-Bulletin* sums it best with this statement from an article published on December 5, 1944, at the beginning of her stardom: "How fate chose Shirley as one in a million for potential fame and fortune is another of those amazing Cinderella stories which happen only in Hollywood.…She was Rochester's gift to Hollywood."

LUCY WILDER AND HER BOOKSTORE

During the 1940s, a common sight in downtown Rochester was a Great Dane walking from a popular bookstore to a nearby bank with a bag of money and receipts clutched gently in his mouth. He was on a mission to make a deposit for the Bookstore of Lucy Wilder. Thor was the beloved canine companion of Lucy Wilder, the bookshop's owner, and it was usually his job to carry the daily deposits to the bank. For locals, not seeing Thor trotting down the sidewalk on his daily errand would've been unusual, but for Mayo Clinic patients and other visitors to the Med City, it was probably a scene that warranted a double take. Located on First Avenue Southwest, the Bookstore of Lucy Wilder was a downtown staple for forty years. Wilder opened it in 1933 after purchasing it from Mabel Ulrich.

Lucy was born Lucy Elizabeth Beeler in Hamilton, Ohio, on May 15, 1889. She married Dr. Russell Wilder in 1911 and lived in Chicago and Vienna, Austria, before moving to Rochester in 1919, when her husband accepted a Mayo Clinic staff position. Wilder's field of expertise was diabetes, and he possessed a dedicated focus on using diet and nutrition as integral parts of medical care in improving patients' health, regardless of their diagnosis. He was nationally acclaimed for his work in this area

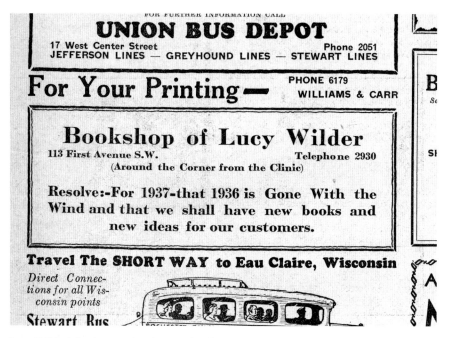

Lucy Wilder's bookstore advertisement in *Know Rochester*, January 1937. *History Center of Olmsted County.*

and for a unique diet prescription restaurant in Rochester. It was created in partnership with Mary Foley, a Mayo Clinic dietitian, and launched in 1922. Wilder and Foley worked closely with the Kahler Corporation to design and implement this new idea in Rochester.

Dr. Wilder and Lucy had two sons, Russell and Thomas, and both became physicians. The Wilders were active members in Rochester society, and Lucy was a member and patron of several organizations, including the College Women's Club, the Salvation Army, the Rochester Arts Association, the League of Women Voters and the YWCA. Lucy was also a founding member of a regular study course held a couple times a month at the Congregational church. The study class had 170 members and held lively discussions on international problems. At a March 4, 1924 meeting, Lucy "gave a very detailed and illuminating review of J.M. Kayne's book, *The Economic Consequences of Peace.*"

When Dr. Wilder retired from the Mayo Clinic in 1950, the Wilders temporarily moved to Washington, D.C., where he worked as head of the National Institute of Arthritis and Metabolic Diseases. For the next three years, Lucy wrote "Capitol Limited," a column about politics and her

Washington, D.C. experiences for the *Mantorville Express* in Dodge County before returning to Rochester permanently. One of her last columns focused on the 1953 U.S. Supreme Court decision on school segregation. She continued to write political commentary after moving back to Rochester with a new column titled "As I See It." An undated *Rochester Post-Bulletin* article called her "brilliant, witty and thorough in her commentary," and her "columns were filled with history of particular pieces of legislation, the goings on at House and Senate Hearings, which she regularly attended, and the voting record of the Minnesota legislators."

While the owner of the Bookstore, Lucy published a book about the Mayo Clinic's history. The 1936 book, *The Mayo Clinic*, was revised several times over twenty years. It is often credited as being the first history book written about the clinic. People gravitated toward the popular store, enjoying not only its selection of books but also its discussions on literature and hot topics of the day. Lucy was by all accounts a charismatic and unique character with outspoken opinions, liberal leanings, an affinity for smoking pipes and an ability to provide a unique retail environment, identified most by Thor, the store's unofficial mascot, a welcoming host. A May 17, 2004 *Rochester Post-Bulletin* article echoed the obituary statement: "The Bookstore became a celebrated gathering spot for intellectual discussions. In the afternoon, Lucy and Dorothy would serve wine and tea until the afternoon's topic was exhausted. Both women were politically active and well-read." Mary "Dorothy" Day was Lucy's longtime friend and business partner.

In addition to selling books, the Bookstore of Lucy Wilder, also called the Bookshop of Lucy Wilder, was home to a popular lending library. Lucy was also quite the cook and baker, and store patrons could depend on being greeted with delicious treats and hot coffee to complement interesting conversation or shelf browsing. There might have been a sample of Lucy's famous "Bishop's Bread," made from a recipe she acquired while living in Vienna. The dessert, more cake than bread, was described in a 1958 *Rochester Post-Bulletin* article as a loaf with "a cracked sugary crust on top, and the sides are smooth and hard. Inside, the creamy yellow loaf is delicately soft textured and flecked with tiny bits of nuts and fruits." Sharing the spotlight with the cake was a forty-year-old mixing gadget Lucy purchased at Chicago's Marshall Field's, which was "a forerunner of the electric mixer, but more versatile, for it not only beats eggs, but grinds coffee, rices potatoes, drips oil for mayonnaise, drop by drop, mixes bread and runs an ice cream freezer. It is several feet tall, and its attachments take up one whole section of Mrs. Wilder's cupboard."

The gravesite of Lucy Wilder and Dorothy Day in Oakwood Cemetery. *Amy Jo Hahn.*

After Dr. Wilder died in 1959, Lucy and Dorothy shared a home until Lucy's death in 1968. Her obituary in the *Rochester Post-Bulletin* called her store "one of the community's intellectual centers and gathering points." Dorothy, who'd been given the store as a gift in 1947, sold it in 1963 to Frank Dougherty. Two years later, Robert Fick took over its ownership. Through the two sales, the store retained its name, but that changed when George Waters bought it in 1975, changing it to Poor Richard Books. The building is no longer standing, as it was torn down and replaced. Dorothy died a year after Lucy, and the two were buried side by side in Rochester's historic Oakwood Cemetery, with Dr. Wilder's grave alongside theirs.

Elizabeth Taylor Greenfield: "The Black Swan"

Located at 301 Broadway Avenue North, the three-story red-brick Avalon Hotel building is one of the Med City's most important historic landmarks. Originally called the Northwestern Hotel, it was built in 1919 by Sam Sternberg and catered to Jewish visitors, providing overnight accommodations and a kosher restaurant during a time when many Jews were denied entrance into hotels and restaurants. In 1944, transplant Verne Manning bought the structure and renamed it the Avalon Hotel. He opened its doors to Black visitors, a majority of whom were Mayo Clinic patients, becoming the first hotel in the city to do so. Many of his guests were famous

Black musicians, entertainers and athletes. But long before the Avalon Hotel cemented its legacy as an important figure in Black history, its address paid host to a famous Black singer, a visit that received enthusiastic acclaim and proved popular enough to deem an encore presentation.

On the evening of October 1, 1863, Broadway House, was filled to bursting with Rochester residents eager to witness a rare performance by the "Black Swan," the stage name of Elizabeth Taylor Greenfield, a famed Black singer who was in the remaining months of her final national tour. Broadway House, the predecessor of the Northwestern and Avalon Hotels, was an important building in Rochester, temporarily serving as the Olmsted County Courthouse while a new building was being constructed. It later fell victim to a fire.

A month before her concert, the September 5 *Rochester City Post* raved about Greenfield's performances in Saint Paul:

> The "Black Swan" has been charming denizens of Saint Paul and vicinity the past few evenings with her inimitable song. Critics who attend her entertainments for the purpose of finding fault are among the first to be melted. They listen, says the Saint Paul Press, and are conquered. Miss Greenfield's peculiarities consist of immense compass, a mellow flexibility of tone and an enunciation that never fails to reach the hearts, as well as the ears, of all listeners.

A few days before her performance, the September 30 *Rochester Republican* encouraged residents to attend with a short paragraph, stating, "If you have a little spare change and wish a good entertainment, go and hear the Black Swan at the Court House tomorrow evening. You will not fail of getting the worth of your money."

Greenfield traveled a difficult road to achieve the aplomb and respect she enjoyed during her 1863 tour. Born as an enslaved girl in Natchez, Mississippi, she was freed, along with her mother, sisters and several others, by her mistress, Mrs. Elizabeth H. Greenfield, after she divorced her plantation-owner husband and moved to Philadelphia, Pennsylvania. By all accounts, Greenfield and her namesake were close, the budding singer choosing to stay with her after her family returned to Africa. Mrs. Greenfield encouraged her singing, leaving a substantial amount of money to her upon death. However, the will was contested, and the "Black Swan" found herself without an income. In addition to her lack of funds, she had difficulty obtaining a musical education due to the color of her skin. But she was determined to pursue a musical career, and her concert's program booklet

MISS ELIZABETH T. GREENFIELD,

THE "BLACK SWAN,"

Will give one Grand Concert prior to her departure for Europe,

At METROPOLITAN HALL, on THURSDAY, 31st March, 1853,

ASSISTED BY

Mdlle. IDA L'ECLUSE, Pianist, from the Royal Conservatoire of Brussels, her
first appearance in this City; Mr. STEPHEN LEACH, and a GRAND
ORCHESTRA Conducted by Mr. G. F. BRISTOW.

Elizabeth Taylor Greenfield, "The Black Swan," 1853 newspaper advertisement. *Public domain.*

gives a detailed biographical sketch (4): "By indomitable perseverance, she surmounted difficulties almost invincible. At first, she taught herself crude accompaniments to her songs, and intuitively perceiving the agreement or disagreement of them, improvised and repeated, until there was heard floating upon the air a very lovely song of one that had a pleasant voice and could play well." She befriended a daughter of prominent physician who agreed to be her accompanist; the two performed at upper-class homes for various social events.

But it wasn't until Greenfield journeyed to Buffalo, New York, on a riverboat that her big break occurred. While aboard, her singing caught the notice of wealthy influential couple who arranged a concert. The *Northwestern Bulletin* wrote on March 5, 1925, that critics "were loud in their acclaim and termed her the 'African Nightingale,' as an offset of Jenny Lind, then at the zenith of her career and called the 'Swedish Nightingale.'" After this introductory performance, Greenfield embarked on a national tour, which included singing at New York City's Metropolitan Hall. She

A view of 301 North Broadway, the location of Broadway House, where Elizabeth Taylor Greenfield performed. *Amy Jo Hahn.*

also traveled across the Atlantic, where "her singing took England by storm. She was commanded to appear before the queen and the nobility, who gave testimony of her wonderful gift. Her trip abroad was a triumph, both artistically and financially."

During her stay in England, Greenfield also studied under Sir George Smart, Queen Victoria's royal organist, at the Royal Academy of Music. During a performance at Stafford House in London, Harriet Beecher Stowe, an enthusiastic attendee, wrote in her *Sunny Memories of Foreign Lands* (101), "The choicest of the elite were there," and Greenfield, performing with several singers, "had a pleasing dark face, wore a black velvet headdress and white carnelian earrings, a black moire antique silk, made high in the neck, with white lace falling sleeves and white gloves. A certain gentleness of manner and self-possession, the result of universal kindness shown her, sat well upon her." Stowe described how Greenfield's voice, "with its keen, searching fire, its penetrating vibrant quality, its *timbre*, as the French have it, cut its way like a Damascus blade to the heart. It was the more touching from occasional rusticities and artistic defects, which showed that she had received no culture from art. She sang the ballad, 'Old Folks at Home,' giving one verse in soprano and the other in the tenor voice." Her switch from soprano to tenor enthralled the crowd, and it "was rapturously encored."

By the time Greenfield gave her 1863 Rochester performance, she was a known entity in the concert scene, and *Rochester City Post* editors applauded her performance in the October 3 edition of the paper: "The concert of the ebony lady at the Court House, on Thursday evening, was fully attended— so much so that Col. Wood, her popular manager, was induced to repeat the entertainment last [Friday] evening, with an entire change of programme, and with a reduction in price of twenty-five cents. It is rare that our people have an opportunity to attend a first-class concert, and when they do, they are not slow in improving their chance."

There was no doubt that Greenfield had impressed Rochester society with her beautiful voice and gained many fans. When she died a decade later at the age of sixty-eight, the *Rochester Post* commented on her death, stating she had been "famous throughout the country," once performing in Rochester. And although the Black Swan never visited the city again, she is intricately woven into the history of Rochester and 301 North Broadway Avenue.

5

WOMEN'S SUFFRAGE ACTIVISTS

SARAH BURGER STEARNS AND JOSEPH ALEXANDER LEONARD

Rochester has the distinction of having the first locally organized suffrage organization in Minnesota. The Rochester Woman's Suffrage Association (RWSA) was founded in 1869, and its founding member would become one of the nation's most influential suffrage leaders. This woman, who first stirred the suffrage pot in Rochester, was a brilliant and educated Michigan transplant who possessed the charisma necessary to persuade people to listen to her ideas and opinions. Her name was Sarah Burger Stearns. Shortly after her arrival in Minnesota, Joseph Alexander Leonard, the *Rochester Post* editor and kindred suffrage supporter, asked Stearns to write for his paper. She accepted, and over the next six years, the two worked as a team, delivering local, state and national suffrage news and editorials to the city.

Joseph Alexander Leonard's Republican newspaper had progressive leanings, and Leonard was an advocate for many political and social agendas, including Black and women's suffrage. His newspaper was filled with articles praising universal suffrage and criticizing the Minnesota legislature on its suffrage failures. Leonard, a physician, lawyer and Republican politician, owned the *Rochester Post* for the next three decades and sat at its helm during the most formative years of Minnesota's equal suffrage fight. The many pro-suffrage articles published in his publication, written by him and Stearns, attested to his leanings regarding women's suffrage. The *Rochester Post*'s articles were especially critical of the Minnesota legislature's continued refusal to

Left: Sarah Burger Stearns. *University of Minnesota Duluth, Kathryn A. Martin Library, Jacoby Studio (Minneapolis, MN).*

Right: Joseph Alexander Leonard. *History Center of Olmsted County.*

pass laws granting women's suffrage and showcased blatant outrage when, in 1869, it awarded suffrage to Black males but did not also extend that right to women.

In addition to Leonard, Stearns found an ally in Dr. Mary Jackman Colburn of Champlin, Minnesota. In January 1867, the two women, along with others called the "friends of equality," petitioned the state legislature for an amendment to the state constitution that would give women the right to vote by removing the word *male* from the voting law's language. The bill died in committee, losing by one vote. Another setback was about to come.

In the first years following the Civil War, Black and women's suffrage advocates worked together to achieve universal suffrage. However, that changed when many white politicians and abolitionists decided to champion Black male suffrage instead. Stearns gave impassioned pleas about striking both the word *white* and *male* from the law, not choosing one over the other. A February 3, 1866 *Rochester Post* article attributed to her says:

We expect to vote for this amendment if it is submitted, because it proposes to strike out the word white, *which never ought to have been in our Constitution, but as we know of no argument for the extension of suffrage that will not apply as well to women as to men, we are sorry that Mr. Mitchell did not strike out the word* male *and make all persons over the age of twenty-two years possessing certain qualifications voters. We can't see why color is not just as good a qualification for voting as sex, nor why a woman is not just as competent to choose a member of the legislature as the negro.*

A December 8, 1866 *Rochester Post* article, most likely written by Stearns (but it could have been written by Leonard), reads: "We hope we may have among the fifty-six Republicans in that body, one of independence enough to propose universal suffrage. It would be just as easy to strike the word *male* from the Constitution at the same time as the word *white*, and there can be no stronger argument in favor of the discrimination in sex than that of color."

After Black men achieved state enfranchisement in 1869, Stearns continued her fight. In November 1869, she posted a notice in the *Rochester Post* about a meeting at her home. The topic: women's suffrage. The discussion resulted in the formation of the RWSA. Stearns wrote the group's mission statement: "Whereas we know many women to feel that, by their votes, they might do much for the help of other women and the good of society, and believe that those thus feel ought to have the privilege of a vote on all matters of public interest; therefore, be it resolved, that we, the undersigned, have associated ourselves together for the purpose of helping to secure this privilege, as soon as possible, to the women of this state." In the following week's paper, she wrote with passion and eloquence in support of women's right to vote:

Woman is subject to a good many wrongs—wrongs partly of her own infliction and also wrongs resulting from the imperfections of our social and business systems and, perhaps, in some respects, from the workings of our political institutions. These wrongs should be redressed, and woman should be emancipated from the bonds imposed by fashion, false education and blind prejudice and brought on to a higher, nobler plane of thought and labor. God has given her a great work to do and has endowed her with ample capacities to perform that work.

Three years later, Stearns and her husband, lawyer and politician Ozora Stearns, moved to Duluth. It was there that Stearns gained national suffrage immortality by serving as vice-president for the Minnesota Association for the Advancement of Women and for the National Woman Suffrage Association. She was also the first president of the Minnesota Woman Suffrage Association.

MARION LOUISA SLOAN

Although Sarah Burger Stearns is Rochester's most famous suffrage activist, Marion Sloan, who arrived in Rochester at the age of ten in 1856, is a close second. Sloan was elected to serve as the Minnesota Woman Suffrage Association's vice-president and was chairman of the first Olmsted County Republican women's organization. Sloan lived to see the ratification of the Nineteenth Amendment and voted for the first time at the age of seventy-four in the 1920 presidential election.

Sloan's thoughts of women's suffrage are referenced in a 1983 *Rochester Post-Bulletin* article, taken from a diary entry: "You say you have all the rights you want, but did you ever think that the lone girl, working alone without the lover to lean upon that you have as not all the rights she wants.…The woman of the future…will she vote?"

Marion Louisa Sloan. *From Mary Dillon Foster's* Who's Who Among Minnesota Women.

Doubtless, she will, for the nation cannot afford to lose so much intellect. It is a minor question."

In her role as MWSA vice-president, Sloan wrote for the *Olmsted County Democrat* about conventions and executive board meetings. Most notable was a 1904 article in which she described the "Woman's Protest Committee on Statehood Letter." Many national women organization leaders signed the letter, encouraging action against a bill that was to come before the Senate Committee of Territories. The bill would combine four western territories into two states. That wasn't the issue. The issue was that the wording of the proposed state's constitutions regarding voting read, "The right of suffrage in these states shall not be restricted nor abridged, save and except on account of illiteracy, minority, sex, convention of felony, mental condition or residence." The protest letter declared this wording an injustice to all women and specifically to "the pioneer women of the West, who have labored and suffered by their husbands' sides to advance civilization, ought not to be so unjustly classed with felons, lunatics and children, while their husbands, equals in other respects, are enfranchised." The letter declares women have been treated unjustly in the past, "but never before has the insult been so open and flagrant, nor has it been an act of Congress." The letter calls for the word *sex* to be removed, because "all persons equally endowed with intelligence are entitled to equal privileges and are under equal obligation to the state." MWSA's executive board voted in favor of supporting the letter and petitioned Minnesota's United States senator Knute Nelson, a member of the Senate Committee of Territories.

Sloan was an active member of Rochester's Universalist church, the Woman's Christian Temperance Union (WTCU) and the Order of the Eastern Star, and she was a teacher and business owner. She shared these ties with many of her sister suffrage activists. The Universalist church and Congregational churches were known for having more progressive stances on various social issues, and the WCTU championed women's suffrage. Rochester had a very active WCTU. Another interesting organization, to which many suffrage supporters belonged, was the Order of the Eastern Star (OES). The order was connected to the Freemasons and had been created by a master mason, Dr. Robert "Rob" Morris, and his wife, Charlotte Mendenhall. It was a fraternal organization open to women and men. It focused on five biblical heroines (Adah, Ruth, Esther, Martha and Electa, the "elect lady" from the Second Epistle of John) and their heroic actions and moral codes. An excerpt from a paper by Dr. Nancy Stearns Theiss states the importance of the OES to women:

> *The Order of the Eastern Star was the first membership organization in the United States that gave women a voice on a national scale. This was an extraordinary accomplishment, given the distance separating the frontier communities from the more populated areas in the United States. The OES gave women a platform of visibility at a time when women had little opportunity in business, government and education. It embodied the power of women as a force to make positive changes in their lives specifically and for women generally. It stood as a beacon for women to get involved locally as well as nationally and internationally to improve society.*

Sloan was an active patron of the order. She served as the Rochester chapter's secretary for twenty-one years.

SARAH WRIGHT CLARK

When Sarah Burger Stearns created the RWSA, the organization's first officers were listed in the *Rochester Post*'s January 22, 1870 issue. Sarah Louise Whitney was president, Sarah Wright Clark and Mrs. M. Moulton shared the vice-president position, the recording secretary was Miss Dora Barrett, the corresponding secretary was Stearns and the treasurer was Mrs. J.W. Keyes, the wife of Grace Universalist Church's reverend. Not much can be found about most of these women. They may have moved away or stopped participating for a variety of reasons, but it was reported in the *Rochester Post* on May 28, 1870, that a small delegation from Rochester attended a national women's suffrage convention in Chicago on May 20. The attendees included Stearns, Whitney, Barrett, Clark and the Reverend J.W. Keyes. The reverend may have attended in support of his wife, as a male chaperone or the paper made a typo and it was actually his wife who attended. The reverend was an ardent supporter of women's suffrage and gave many lectures supporting the cause.

Although the other officers, with the exception of Stearns, seemed to have vanished from newspaper accounts, a little more is known of Clark, whose husband was a surveyor, businessman and Rochester mayor. Clark, like Sloan, was active in Rochester's Universalist church and was a leading WCTU member. The May 9, 1874 *Rochester Post* reported that Clark attended a city council meeting, presenting a petition with 1,158 signatures (518 men and 640 women), asking that "no license for the sale of intoxicating drinks be granted for the ensuing year." She became a widowed landowner in 1876 and was unhappy with paying high property taxes without the power to participate in decisions about taxing. She petitioned the State of Minnesota "for removal of her political disabilities [not being able to vote] or exemption from taxation." Her request echoed the American Revolution's rebellion cry: "No taxation without representation!" Clark owned a corset shop along Broadway Avenue. She didn't just own the shop; she made the corsets, a respected corsetiere. An 1883 *Rochester Post* listing under "Local Items" says, "We call attention to the corsets made by Mrs. J.B. Clark. They are said to be equal in every respect to the very best. Ladies will do well to examine them." An April 2016 *Rochester Post-Bulletin* article about the Universalist Unitarian church quoted from her 1891 obituary: "Her habits of industry never languished."

JULIA CUTSHALL

It is unknown what happened to the Rochester Woman Suffrage Association. After organizing, it was agreed that the group would have meetings on the first Saturday of every month in Good Templar Hall, which was located on the second floor of a new brick building called "Whiting Block." The available historic newspapers make no clear mention of the RWSA again after May 1870, when RWSA officers attended the Chicago suffrage convention. What is recorded is that thirty years after the RWSA's creation, a new county suffrage organization was formed. A convention resulting in the creation of the Olmsted County Equal Suffrage Association was held from September 21 to September 22 at Grace Universalist Church.

Miss Laura Gregg, a leading Midwest suffragist, attended, as did Universalist reverend Ida Hultin. The September 29, 1899 *Olmsted County Democrat* described Hultin's topic as "along the line of influence of the women in the training of children and the rights of the mothers to the ballot," and it said she "did not ask for enfranchisement as a favor, but as a right that women were entitled to by the law of common sense and morality." The article states it was "one of the best [papers] during the convention, and she was the recipient of many expressions of approval and appreciation by the audience."

Rochester resident Julia Irish Cutshall stood out from the crowd of attendees. Cutshall read the first paper of the convention, titled "Do Women Know Enough to Vote?" The *Olmsted County Democrat* complimented the paper, stating it "was a very informative one and clearly proved that women are as well qualified for the franchise as the stronger sex," with Cutshall clearly presenting her arguments, making "a very good impression." The *Record and Union* agreed Cutshall "proved from her standpoint that they do, and also, that if women could vote, politics would be thereby purified." Cutshall was elected as the organization's first president. Its other officers were Laura Amsteadt, vice-president; Emma Peck, secretary; Jennie Allen, treasurer; and Mrs. John Yates, auditor. Little is known what happened following the convention, but she was a longtime member of the Congregational church, its adored organist until she moved to Minneapolis in 1909.

AMELIA HATFIELD WITHERSTINE

Amelia Hatfield Witherstine.
From Rochester Daily Post and
Record, *June 3, 1916, History
Center of Olmsted County.*

Two years after Cutshall exited the Rochester scene, Amelia Hatfield Witherstine made history on March 14, 1911, by becoming the first woman elected to the Rochester School Board. She would serve on the board for twelve years, spending most of those years as its president. When Witherstine was selected by the Women's Civic League as its candidate, the *Olmsted County Democrat* reported, "The league could scarcely have made a better choice for a lady commissioner. Mrs. Witherstine is a woman of much common sense; her mind is analytical and her judgment good. Though progressive, she is not a faddist. She is well educated, a splendid home-maker and a brilliant club-woman."

Witherstine was also the first woman to serve on an Olmsted County District Court jury and was the president of Rochester's WCTU for twenty-five years. She was honored on December 11, 1937, for over fifty years of service to the WCTU; she was a member for sixty-two years. As a WCTU member, she was a delegate to a national convention that was held in Cincinnati in 1903 and hosted many meetings at her home. She was also a member of the Congregational church, the American Legion's president and a member of the Order of the Eastern Star. Her husband, Dr. Horace Witherstine, served as Rochester's mayor from 1892 to 1895, 1896 to 1897 and 1902 to 1903. In a March 27, 1920 *Rochester Daily Post and Record* article titled "Ten Years Ago," she is mentioned as stating she "believed the principle [women's suffrage] right but was doubtful that women would take advantage of it."

EMMA POTTER ALLEN

Emma Potter Allen moved to Rochester in 1896. She wasted little time in joining several local women's organizations and served as the president of the Civic League for several years. She was also a longtime member of the WCTU and the Order of the Eastern Star. Under her leadership, the

Civic League helped elect Amelia Hatfield Witherstine to the school board, hired a full-time public health officer and a woman police officer. She was integral to the success of many public health and social service initiatives in Rochester. Allen began her work with the Minnesota Federation of Women's Clubs in 1910, and she was the First District's treasurer, vice-president and president.

In September 1919, as president of the Minnesota Federation of Women's Clubs, she worked closely with the Minnesota Woman Suffrage Association to organize a grand celebration on the state capitol's lawn on September 8, the opening day of a special legislative session in which Minnesota would become the fifteenth state to ratify the Nineteenth Amendment to the United States Constitution.

In anticipation of the momentous event, Allen penned a letter to club chapter presidents across the state, encouraging them to journey to Saint Paul on this historical occasion. In a September 3 local newspaper article, Allen stated, "Minnesota women will storm the state capitol building for ratification of equal suffrage by the legislature of Minnesota." According to the September 3, 1919 *Willmar Tribune*, the event was to be "the greatest celebration of rejoicing ever attempted by the women of the state," and a "decorated booth will be erected in the rotunda of the capitol at Saint Paul, where out-of-town women will register and receive yellow flowers for decoration and where directions will be given them for the events of the day. The galleries and corridors will be thronged with women from early in the morning until ratification takes place." Following the ratification, Allen was one of the attendees of a celebratory banquet at the Saint Paul Hotel, and she was also an honored guest at what was coined the "Victory Dinner" in November 1919. Also in November, she was elected to an advisory committee for the newly created Minnesota League of Women Voters and spoke at a league meeting at the schoolhouse in Stewartville. The *Rochester Daily Post and Record* reported, "Mrs. George Allen of Rochester, state president of the Federation of Women's Clubs, gave an interesting address, calling the women 'fellow citizens' and urging them to consider it a sacred duty to use the ballot wisely."

Emma Potter Allen. *From Mary Dillon Foster's* Who's Who Among Minnesota Women.

Stella Doran Cussons

Stella Doran Cussons of Stewartville presided over that November 1919 league meeting where Allen was a guest speaker. Cussons was a teacher and member of the Stewartville Board of Education for three years. Cussons was also the president of the State Federation of Women's Clubs, First District, and actively involved in the WCTU. She, too, was a member of the Order of the Eastern Star. After the ratification of the Nineteenth Amendment, she was a delegate to the 1920 Republican county, district and state conventions, becoming one of the state's first women to do so. While attending the State Republican Party Convention in March 1920, Cussons delivered an enthusiastic nomination speech for Carrie Jorgens Fosseen to attend as a delegate to the party's national convention that was to be held in Chicago from June 8 to June 12. This marked the first time in state history that a woman was recognized on a state Republican convention floor. Fosseen attended the Chicago convention, where she marked another historical first. According to *Who's Who Among Minnesota Women*, "Mrs. Fosseen was the first woman delegate at large to be elected to the United States and the first woman to be given the floor at the National Republican Convention. She was one of the four women to be named to the Rules Committee…and was one of eight women appointed on the executive committee of the National Republican Committee.…During the national campaign of 1920, she was co-chairman of the National Speaker's Bureau."

Before the National Republican Convention, Fosseen gave speeches about the Republican Party and its positions to women's groups across the state. Her busy itinerary included a stop in Rochester. On Saturday, April 24, Fosseen appeared at the Olmsted County Courthouse, most likely at the invitation of Cussons, who held her is such obviously high esteem. Upon announcing her upcoming lecture, the *Daily Post and Record* declared:

> *After long years of hard work, anxious waiting, much thought, time and money expended, at last women have come into their birthright and are welcomed by the men as truly helpers in the political field. Women may vote. Note then, women all, is the time to demonstrate that we are capable, anxious and very willing to do so by becoming interested in all the questions of the day, reading about them, discussing them, thinking about them. In short, give some time to the subject and the privilege.*

JESSIE VAN SCHAICK PREDMORE

Jessie Van Schaick Predmore, a Rochester native, worked alongside Allen and Cussons as a member of the Minnesota Federation of Women's Clubs. She participated in various conservation efforts and the improvement and management of local roads and highways and was an active member of the American Red Cross, the YWCA and the WCTU. She was also the first president of the Olmsted County Farm Bureau. In addition, she served on the Rochester School Board and was actively involved in county child welfare initiatives.

One of Predmore's most notable activities was serving as the Olmsted County chairman of the Liberty Loan Campaign, which collected thousands of bonds during World War I. In fact, so impressive was her bond haul that she received a personal letter from Eleanor Wilson McAdoo, the wife of U.S. Treasury Secretary William G. McAdoo and national chairman of the campaign. The letter praised Predmore's work and declared, "The results of the last campaign have more than justified the belief of the Treasury Department in the ability of women to stand shoulder to shoulder with men in organizing and conducting the campaigns for the sale of Liberty bonds and in their right to the title 'equal partners.'" Predmore also received a letter from Frances T. Chamberlain, a state chairman, that read, "I cannot thank you enough for your prompt and business-like reports....In all events, you have covered the county splendidly, and I want you to know what a help it is to us to have had the work handled as it has been." Predmore was also one of the women who expressed her opinion on women's suffrage in the August 19, 1920 *Rochester Daily Post and Record* article. She stated, "I am for the amendment. I wanted the privilege of voting, even if I don't use it. It seemed a degradation to be denied the franchise together with Indians and the rest. I shall take advantage of the privilege; however, I have not decided on my party."

6

The Headliners

Clara Cook Kellogg: International Hostess

Although many Minnesotans are aware of the main thoroughfare called Kellogg Boulevard in downtown Saint Paul, some probably don't know the importance of the man the street honors. And most Rochester residents no longer remember that the busy street and a local middle school are named after a hometown farm boy turned lawyer who navigated national and international political waters, authoring a peace pact that awarded him a Nobel Peace Prize. His career was impressive and his accolades were plenty, but it was his wife whom he turned to, not making any career decisions without her input and lovingly acknowledging her influence on his success. She would ascend societal heights with him, becoming a celebrated hostess in Washington, D.C., and London—even becoming friends with a queen.

That man was Frank Billings Kellogg. He immigrated with his family to Olmsted County at the age of nine. His wife was Clara Cook. They were married on June 16, 1886, in Rochester. Clara was a quiet, shy twenty-five-year-old schoolteacher, and Frank was a thirty-year-old charismatic and ambitious lawyer who'd quickly amass a small fortune in private law and gain national and international fame and respect in the political arena. Young Clara Cook could not have imagined where her life would lead her when she accepted Frank's proposal, but she was probably slightly in awe of her fiancé's seemingly endless energy, intelligence and goals for the future. And Frank no doubt saw in his new wife a brilliant woman with a kind and

Left: Clara Cook Kellogg, 1905. *U.S. Library of Congress, Harris & Ewing.*

Right: Frank Billings Kellogg, 1900. *U.S. Library of Congress, National Photography Company Collection.*

unassuming nature; her beauty, elegance and vibrant personality attracted others like a moth to a flame, even if she considered herself to be rather bookish and introverted.

For three years, the couple lived an uneventful and peaceful life in her hometown, where Frank practiced law as a partner in the firm of Kellogg and Eaton with Burt W. Eaton. However, it wasn't long before Frank's reputation as a tenacious, dedicated and gregarious lawyer reached beyond the boundaries of southeast Minnesota. This was in large part owed to his appearance before the U.S. Supreme Court, arguing in defense of three local communities against a railroad company for lost compensation. His win in the nation's highest court also won him an offer at a law firm in Minneapolis. It was an offer Frank and Clara couldn't pass up, so they left their families, friends and colleagues for the big city, and Frank began to work at the newly named Davis, Kellogg and Severance. The "Kellogg Send-off" was held on October 7, 1887, at the Cook Hotel, complete with a banquet and live orchestra, and it included eighty-four of the couple's closest friends and local business owners. Leaving was bittersweet for the couple, and they would continue to correspond with their families and friends with an occasional visit as they climbed the social ladder. In 1909, Frank returned to address area farmers, emphasizing his great love for the community of his and Clara's youth; the address was recorded by the *Olmsted County Democrat* on October 8, 1909:

> *The commencement of my life's work was among this people, upon the farm; my principal education was in the district school; and of the little that I have accomplished in the great world, much is due to the training and self-reliance I there received the kindly feeling and goodwill of the people of this county. The love and respect of one's neighbors and their desire for one's success is a bulwark in the great battle of life. Believe me, in the years that have passed since I left this community I have ever carried with grateful memories of your loyalty and kindness, and I am every ready to pay tribute to the splendid citizenship of Olmsted County.*

In his new role, Frank represented large corporations, with business interests in steel and iron and railroads. And even though Frank gained a reputation as a corporate lawyer, President Theodore Roosevelt selected him to be on his team of "trust busters," who were focused on bringing suits against large conglomerates that had become powerful monopolies and breaking them apart. This success garnered him national fame, and before long, he'd won a U.S. Senate seat, which led to his appointment as a United States ambassador to the United Kingdom, followed by a four-year term as secretary of state under President Calvin Coolidge.

Clara's star rose with her husband's, and she "joined her efficient hands with his in the handcraft of a great career" (Rogers, 172—*American Bar Leaders: Biographies of the Presidents of the American Bar Association, 1878-1928*). Her October 2, 1942 *Rochester Post-Bulletin* obituary declared, "As her husband's legal career advanced him to prominence as an ambassador to London and secretary of state, Mrs. Kellogg's unusual talent and ability as a gracious hostess became known. Her husband frequently attributed his successes to her counsel and to her assistance as hostess to groups with whom he came in contact…a hostess with international renown." She gained stardom among world leaders and Great Britain's politicians and upper-crust aristocracy from the moment she stepped onto the societal pages with her first reception at Crewe House in London, "one of the striking residences of the West End, where Mrs. Kellogg held open house weekly, in addition to frequent elaborate social affairs" (*Rochester Post-Bulletin*, December 22, 1937). Her popularity only grew when Queen Mary received her at the Court of St.

Queen Mary of Teck, queen consort of the United Kingdom, 1915. *U.S. Library of Congress, George Grantham Bain Collection.*

James, the two taking an instant liking to each other. Although not much has been written about their friendship, an undated *Rochester Daily Bulletin* article said the Queen of England gave Clara a parting gift, recognizing their bond: "The brooch, which the queen sent to Mrs. Kellogg with a note in her own handwriting, is fashioned of gold and contains three large amethysts and a pearl. It has been a favorite ornament of Her Majesty for years, and the giving of it, in addition to the usual expressions of regret and courtesy, signifies a distinct personal regard of the queen for Mrs. Kellogg." So notable was this royal friendship that the *Rochester Post-Bulletin* made mention of it in Clara's obituary, stating she was "considered one of the most beloved American women at the Court of St. James."

After his appointment as ambassador, Frank served as secretary of state for several years, and the couple made their home in the nation's capital. It was during his tenure in this position that Frank cemented his name in the history books by coauthoring a treaty with French ambassador Aristide Briand. In 1928, the two ambassadors worked together to obtain agreement from over fifty countries to renounce wars of aggression. The Pact of Paris, known as the Kellogg-Briand Pact, but officially titled "The General Treaty for Renunciation of War as an Instrument of National Policy," awarded Frank the Nobel Peace Prize in 1929. It would provide the legal foundation for the trials of World War II against German and Japanese leaders.

Frank's success in his role as secretary of state and his Nobel Peace Prize win garnered him a prestigious appointment to the World Court in the Hague. After deteriorating health forced Frank to leave the court, he and Clara chose to return to the home they built in 1889 at 633 Fairmont in Saint Paul. They hoped to enjoy a long retirement together. However, that was not meant to be, and within three years, Clara was a widow. Frank was entombed at the Washington National Cathedral in Washington, D.C., and Clara would join him five years later.

Although several prominent men, including President Franklin D. Roosevelt and Drs. William and Charles Mayo, paid tribute to Kellogg upon his death, Clara's importance to his stellar career should not be overlooked. Many biographies written about Kellogg make mention of his respect, admiration and love for Clara; how they shared a marriage of true partnership; and that Clara was a strong influence on Frank's personal and professional decisions. Kellogg was known to graciously compliment his wife often in the public arena, even stating that President Coolidge appointed him ambassador "as much because of Mrs. Kellogg as for himself." Upon Clara's death, *TIME* magazine noted, "She was a tactful, patient woman whose grace often counteracted her husband's impulsive conversation."

And when Clara's ashes were placed next to Frank's in the National Cathedral, together again side by side, as they had been in life, a stone etching was made to proclaim how important she had been to this dedicated American statesman:

Behind this stone are the ashes of
1856—Frank Billings Kellogg—1937
and of
1861—Clara Cook Kellogg—1942
his beloved wife

Richard Warren Sears and the Conley Camera Co.

Richard Warren Sears, the founder of the Sears, Roebuck and Co. and the brilliant mind behind its famous mail order catalogue, has a connection to

Richard Warren Sears Home, Stewartville. *Amy Jo Hahn.*

Rochester and Olmsted County. Sears was born in Stewartville, Olmsted County, on December 7, 1863, to James and Eliza Burton. By the time Richard was seven years old, his family was living in Spring Valley, Fillmore County. Sears's childhood friends included Almanzo Wilder, the husband of children's book author Laura Ingalls Wilder, and the Conley brothers, Kerry and Frederick, the eventual founders and owners of the Conley Camera Company. It was this friendship that connected Sears to Rochester's entrepreneurial spirit.

Richard's father died when he was a young man, leaving the family in severe debt due to his poor investments, and Richard became responsible for supporting his mother and sisters. His quest for a steady paycheck led him to an early career with the railroad, taking jobs as a telegraph operator and station agent. While a station agent in Redwood Falls, Minnesota, Richard discovered a shipment of watches a jewelry dealer refused to accept. Sears decided he could sell them—and he did, quite successfully. This business venture set him down a new career path selling the timepieces. He moved to Minneapolis and started a mail order catalogue business called the R.W. Sears Watch Company. His ambitions led him to move his company to Chicago. He soon partnered with Alvah Roebuck, a watchmaker, and in 1893, they formed the Sears, Roebuck and Co. Their mail order product line began with watches, diamonds and jewelry, but it soon expanded to include a variety of product offerings. The catalogue became popular for rural customers who lived far away from big city stores. Despite his move to the Windy City and the national growth of his business, Sears didn't forget about his friends back home.

The Conley brothers had started their own business in their hometown. They owned a store that sold jewelry, watches and eyeglasses, but with the arrival of the Eastman Kodak Camera in 1888, the brothers saw an opportunity to design and build their own line of cameras and accessories. They established the Conley Camera Company in 1899. Sears took an immediate interest in the brothers' inventions and offered to sell their products through his mail order business. Soon, the Conley Camera Company outgrew its modest headquarters in Spring Valley. The brothers, following the shrewd advice and guidance of Sears, who certainly saw much potential in his friends' company, moved to Rochester in 1904. They moved into a building at 14 Fourth Street Southwest that previously housed a clothing manufacturer, which allowed them to make a smooth transition and gave them the ability to keep up production. The company continued to grow after being awarded several patents for camera parts and accessories.

When Eastman Kodak bought the Rochester Optical and Camera Co., another camera supplier to Sears, Roebuck and Co., Sears stepped in to give his old friends a marketplace advantage, making the executive decision to sell only Conley Cameras in his catalogue. The cameras and their accompanying parts would be sold exclusively through Sears, Roebuck and Co., which had gained acclaim as the "world's largest mail order house." The cameras would be sold under the name Seroco, a name given to all cameras listed in the Sears catalogue. Seroco was a Sears, Roebuck and Co. creation, an acronym devised from the company's name. This deal was also advantageous to Sears, as he was agitated by a change in business dealings with camera companies he'd worked with previously. In a full-page advertisement in the 1908 *Sears, Roebuck and Co. Catalogue*, Sears wrote to his consumers about the change. His company had worked for several years with eastern camera manufacturers in business arrangements

The Conley Camera Factory building. *Amy Jo Hahn.*

that were mutually beneficial, but a recent development had soured that partnership. Sears wrote, "The Camera Trust, having become more and more powerful, forced the manufacturer of the Seroco cameras to sell out, and as soon as they acquired control of this factory, together with all other camera factories, they refused to furnish us with cameras unless we would allow them to dictate to us the prices at which we should sell them" (672). He wrote of his childhood friends in the advertisement:

> *We knew them to be men of great ability as manufacturers—men whose knowledge of camera making was second to none, and we entered into an arrangement with these gentlemen to build and operate for us a big, modern, complete camera factory, a factory whose entire resources should be devoted to making Seroco cameras, making us absolutely independent of the trust and enabling us to sell better cameras at lower prices than we had ever been able to do in the past—better cameras at one-half the prices that the ordinary trust dealer is compelled to charge.*

Sears continued praising this new venture, claiming the cameras were better quality that anything they'd sold before, and "every year since we went into the new factory, [it] has seen improvements in the way of new

Richard Warren Sears, 1900. *U.S. Library of Congress, Sears, Roebuck and Company.*

and special machinery, better facilities and increased skill on the part of the various operatives throughout the factory." Five years after the Rochester move, the Conley brothers and Sears built a new factory. Sears helped finance the project by purchasing a large portion of the company. As part of the arrangement, the Seroco name was dropped, and the Conley name was placed on the products. By November 1910, Sears, Roebuck and Co. bought complete interest in the camera company. The Conley brothers moved on to different ventures, with Kerry remaining in Rochester and Frederick moving to Oregon.

The Conley Camera Co. became the Conley Co. in 1932, its name changed since it no longer manufactured cameras. The company focused on making phonographs and record players throughout the next seven decades. The Conley Co. was sold in 1940, becoming Waters Conley Co., and the Conley name would eventually disappear through other company mergers.

Richard Sears died on September 28, 1914. The company he founded continued to flourish for several decades. Its first brick-and-mortar store was built in 1925, and it would own the title as the largest retailer in the United States for many years. Its last store closed its doors in 2022. Its mail order business, the creation of Richard Sears, ended in 1993, one hundred years after he and Roebuck officially began Sears, Roebuck and Co.

HUGH LINCOLN COOPER: HYDROELECTRIC ENGINEER

Rochester's electricity is provided by the Lake Zumbro Hydroelectric Generating Plant, which is located a few miles north of the city on the Zumbro River in Wabasha County. The plant is listed in the National Register of Historic Places due to its connection with the brilliant engineer who designed it, Hugh Lincoln Cooper. Cooper was born in a small hamlet in Houston County but apprenticed in Rochester before quickly moving onward and upward to take charge of designing and constructing many premier examples of hydroelectric power across the country and the world.

Cooper was the son of a flourmill owner. He grew up in Sheldon, Minnesota, about eighty minutes southeast of Rochester. After graduating from Rushford High School in 1883, he was determined to embark on a career building bridges. He discovered his passion while helping a neighbor build a forty-foot wooden bridge over a small creek. He worked on bridges in Wisconsin for the Chicago, Milwaukee and Saint Paul Railroad for a couple of years before landing a position with Rochester's Horace Ebenezer Horton.

Cooper had applied many times to Horton's company and had been turned down, but finally, his persistence paid off. Perhaps Horton saw a bit of himself in the boy. After all, Horton mirrored the same passion for building as young Cooper and had spent the last twenty years of his life perfecting his engineering skills and working hard to gain a respected reputation as a bridge builder. Horton built his first bridge in 1867; it was an arched wood structure spanning 126 feet across the Zumbro River in Oronoco. Horton tested Cooper, sending him to work on a bridge project in Wisconsin during a harsh winter for $1.59 a day. Horton was positive Cooper would give up on bridge building after spending weeks working in brutally cold conditions as a common laborer. But he was wrong. Cooper's interest in the business and his determination to succeed only intensified. The young man impressed Horton with his skills, engineering knowledge and work ethic. Horton's company did significant work, and one of their projects was constructing the cantilever deck-truss Wabasha Street Bridge in Saint Paul. Horton appointed Cooper as the project manager. Overseeing the construction was an important milestone for Cooper.

While Cooper worked diligently on perfecting the Wabasha Street Bridge, Horton focused on bigger opportunities. He was determined to grow his company, and in 1889, he got his wish. The successful construction of his Dubuque High Bridge over the Mississippi River gained him reputable notice on a national scale, and he pursued a merger between his company and the Kansas City Bridge and Iron Company to form the Chicago Bridge and Iron Works Company. He selected his young protégé as the superintendent and chief engineer. Cooper would only stay in the position for a few years before a relatively new field sparked his interest: hydroelectric engineering. He soon left Horton's employment, informing the president of a Dayton, Ohio company that manufactured wind turbines and hydroelectric equipment that he going to work for him. He insisted on working for nothing so he could gain experience in the new field. It wasn't long before he was on the payroll. This was followed by an appointment as assistant chief engineer. A 1929 *Rochester Post-Bulletin* reprint of an undated *New York Times* article claimed he was "a vivid and arresting figure...a blunt, square-cut person, who carries himself with something of abrupt confidence of a fighting cock. With him, a thought instantly generates energy, and he goes into action smoothly as one of his own dynamos." His tireless pursuit of opportunities in a hydroelectric career certainly echoes this ambitious personality. After his stint at the Stilwell-Bierce and Smith-Vaile Company, Cooper worked as an engineering consultant, building hydroelectric dams in North and South America, Jamaica and the West Indies.

At the beginning of the twentieth century, Cooper started the Hugh L. Cooper Company, which was based out of New York. He supervised the building of the 1906 Toronto Power Generating Station located just above the powerful Niagara Falls, successfully harnessing the Niagara River's waterpower to provide electricity to Toronto, Ontario. Cooper tackled new hydroelectric challenges by supervising power plant projects on larger, wider and slower rivers. According to the Lake Zumbro Hydroelectric Generating Plant's National Register of Historic Places application, "Cooper was among the first hydroelectric engineers to successfully exploit relatively small drops in major rivers, which, because of their great width, flowage and susceptibility to flooding, posed enormous engineering challenges. Cooper's hallmark was the extended, straight-created, concrete gravity dam with wide, overflow spillway and integral powerhouse."

He first applied this new construction design to the McCalls Ferry Dam, now called the Holtwood Hydroelectric Plant, across the Susquehanna River on the border of Pennsylvania and Maryland. The project was started in 1905 and took five years to complete. Cooper improved on this new design when constructing the Keokuk Power Plant, commonly referred to Lock and Dam No. 19 and run by the U.S. Army Corps of Engineers. Its construction began in 1910 and was completed in 1913. The 53-foot-high, 4,696-foot-long dam was built across the Mississippi River between Keokuk, Iowa, and Hamilton, Illinois. It would hold the title as the world's largest hydroelectric plant until Cooper's Wilson Dam in Muscle Shoals, Alabama, on the Tennessee River surpassed it in 1924. In between these two massive projects, Cooper took time to return to Rochester to survey for a hydroelectric plant at the city's request.

It was quite a big deal for Rochester to acquire such a prestigious engineer to design its hydroelectric plant, which was much smaller than the projects Cooper was known for. However, Cooper never cut ties with Rochester or lost his affection for the city or the whole of southeastern Minnesota. He still had family in the area. His wife's parents lived in the city. He'd met Fanny Graves while working for Horton. Fanny's father, Albert, owned a livery business there and was active in the horse racing circuit. Fanny was known to be an excellent horsewoman, often taking her father's prized racing colts and fillies for rides around town. An undated biographical sketch written about the Coopers commented on Fanny's equine skills: "Fanny Graves could handle any horse in her father's stable. One day, when she was driving one of the most spirited ones, it ran away with her and threw her out of the phaeton. As soon as a passerby could catch the animal, she climbed back into the carriage and, in spite of injuries, drove home alone. Regardless of all protests, she went right on driving the mettlesome young racer that might have killed her. This was the kind of girl who cast her lot with Rochester's rising young engineer."

Fanny was described as being petite and blond. Fanny was also musically gifted. She graduated from the Northwestern Conservatory of Music in Saint Paul in June 1891; she was also awarded the school's Medal of Honor for her piano talent and earned a certificate for her skill with the instrument. In October 1892, she married Cooper, and the two spent their honeymoon roughing it at one of his project sites in Spokane, Washington. They camped in sparse accommodations with little to no amenities and Fanny had no other female companionship. Throughout their marriage, Fanny would accompany Cooper to many other work sites. Fanny had courage, stamina, intelligence and an adventurous spirit, which made her a good match for the highly energetic and constantly roving Cooper. She was once reported to have crossed a canyon on a cable that was used to deliver supplies to one of Cooper's job sites.

Cooper submitted a design for the Lake Zumbro Hydroelectric Generating Plant, and the city awarded him a contract with construction provided by the Omaha Structural Steel Bridge Company in the spring of 1917. Construction began that summer. Cooper was designated the project's main supervisor, but when the United States entered World War I and he enlisted, he left engineers H.H. Dimow and John Hall in charge of completing the construction of the concrete structure. The Lake Zumbro Hydroelectric Generating Plant was crafted in the Greek Revival style and was completed in 1919. It is a straight-crested gravity dam with an attached powerhouse and room for three hydroelectric generating units each with a 1,350-horespower turbine, although only two were installed. The dam, spanning 440-feet and reaching 60 feet in height, created Lake Zumbro, a now popular recreational destination.

During the war, Cooper worked in the U.S. Army Corps of Engineers. He was stationed as a chief engineer in Bordeaux, France, where he was in charge of preparing the busy port on the Garonne River for the arrival of thousands of American soldiers, supplies and military equipment. Due to his contributions and accomplishments during the war, Cooper returned home a decorated veteran and then with the title of colonel before his name.

In addition to consulting on the Lake Biwa project in Japan and Egypt's Aswan Dam on the Nile River, Cooper was recruited by the Soviet Union in 1926 to survey for an eight-hundred-thousand-horsepower hydroelectric station in what is now Ukraine. After submitting an initial survey report, the Russian government hired him to supervise the construction of the Dnieper Hydroelectric Station or Dnesprostroi Dam. The massive project was completed in 1932. For his contribution to this important project, Russia awarded Cooper the Order of the Red Banner of Labour, the Soviet Union's third-highest civil award. This masterpiece of hydroelectric power was destroyed during World War II in order to keep the German army from crossing the river.

Cooper died in 1937 in Stamford, Connecticut. His life was an industrious compilation of engineering feats and historically recognized architectural structures around the nation and the world. Yet for all his prestigious acclaim, "Despite his zest in the work itself, of his love of a problem solved and a struggle

The construction of the Lake Zumbro Hydroelectric Generating Plant. *History Center of Olmsted County.*

Lake Zumbro Hydroelectric Generating Plant. *History Center of Olmsted County.*

won, he finds his greatest satisfaction not in those very human delights but in the vastly broader contemplation of the car which carries a tired woman to her home, the radio which brings music to shut-ins, the electric light which brighten the smallest village and the current that turns household machinery and lightens the burden of farm women—all these bring a sense of work worth doing to the man whose job has been that of creating the power that runs them" (*New York Times* and *Rochester Post-Bulletin*, April 26, 1929).

And even though he possessed a reputation for being blunt and outspoken, Cooper excelled at project management, showing a remarkable natural ability to lead construction, engineering and laborer divisions as one ambitious and determined team, together completing astounding hydroelectric marvels. The *New York Times* lauded him with well-deserved and earned praise:

> *Born in the Middle West before there was such a thing as hydroelectric engineering, he has grown up with his profession, and he and it have contributed to each other's development. Starting with no resources but determination and no education but that of a small town's school, he has become a recognized genius of waterpower, called into consultation by great corporations and national governments. A list of the rivers with which he has worked reads like a roster of power sources.*

Beyond being deeply logical, analytical and scientific, with the left-brain dominance needed for his type of work, Cooper said his passions for drama, music and all arts were contributing factors to his professional achievements. He believed great engineers had one thing in common: creativity. When the New York Times asked him to share how to be successful in his profession, he said, "If I told you that the foremost requisite for a successful engineer was imagination, you wouldn't believe it. But it's true."

BELVA SNODGRASS: BELOVED EDUCATOR

When Belva Snodgrass died in 1983, the May 13 issue of the *Rochester Post-Bulletin* ran her obituary prominently, beginning it with this complimentary introduction: "Belva Snodgrass, whose name was synonymous with education in Rochester, died Wednesday."

Belva was ninety-two at the time of her death and had been gone from Rochester for several years after returning to her home state of Indiana. She died in a nursing home, of which she'd been a resident since 1975. Belva was widely regarded as one of the community's most popular educators. Only two years before, she'd made local newspaper and television headlines when a passionate campaign led by former students sought to name a new school in her honor. The school eventually took the name Willow Creek, a name Snodgrass most likely approved of more than her own. She was known to have chuckled at the idea that a school would use her name. She said in a *Rochester Post-Bulletin* interview, "There's always been wise-cracking about my name." And she supposedly once declared, "No child wants to attend a school named Snodgrass." Despite the self-deprecating humor revolving around her name, she expressed how grateful she was for the love and support from former pupils and the community. "The letters of appreciation, the notes and telephone calls mean more to me than the naming of any building," she told the newspaper.

Her career in the Rochester Public School System began in 1922, when she was hired as a teacher. By 1925, she had moved into the administration, and over the next three decades, she held positions as a dean of students, a junior and senior high school principal and a director of student accounting. Snodgrass was actively involved in every part of students' learning and worked diligently to improve class curriculum, including that in college preparatory courses. She was an adamant supporter and advocate for fellow teachers and their classroom work. The *Rochester Post-*

Belva Snodgrass. *History Center of Olmsted County, Clarence Stearns, photographer (Rochester, MN).*

Bulletin obituary commented, "As an administrator, Snodgrass was popular among teachers, perhaps because of her oft-stated conviction that the classroom teacher 'is the key person of the school.'" It was obvious she was held in high esteem by her colleagues, but remarkably, that respect and admiration carried over to the teenagers under her care and tutelage. She was tough. She was strict. She was feared. She was revered. But the repeated refrain from students was that she was committed to ultimate fairness. She was always consistently fair. When the boys were caught being mischievous, they agreed that they deserved the punishment she bestowed. No one wanted to be a disappointment to Ms. Snodgrass.

She tried to turn punishments into positive learning experiences, even going as far as to start a yearly Halloween party for the city's youth after several were caught being hooligans around town, resulting in severe vandalism to personal and business properties. The annual bash gave the kids something else to do, and police reported a significant reduction in pranks and property damages. When deciding what her school's role should be in the teenagers' crime spree, Snodgrass stated to the local media, "The idea that Halloween is a time to insult your neighbors and friends cannot be tolerated."

She was compassionate, kind and forgiving when the occasion called for it. In an article written by Harley Flathers for the May 12, 2012 *Rochester Post-Bulletin*, a previous student shared his memory of how she brought schoolwork to his home after his mother died, gushing, "Belva was just wonderful." Another student told Flathers, "Belva was a good person—no goofing off, tough, but friendly and fair." She purchased boys' graduation suits with her own money when she knew a family couldn't afford them, and she personally visited the homes of kids who dropped out of school and encouraged them to return. She also established a mentor program between new students and older students to help improve educational success.

A *Rochester Post-Bulletin* editorial written to celebrate Rochester mayor Dewy Day's declaration that Belva's birthday, October 20, 1971, was "Belva Snodgrass Day," offered the following comment on her reputation:

> *A strong disciplinarian, she demanded and usually got the best out of her students. When you were called on the carpet in her office, you remembered it for a variety of reasons, but most of all, it remained a lasting impression because ultimately, the student realized that her discipline, although tough, was always fair and just. In everything she did, she placed the interest of the students and the school first in her heart and mind.*

On the evening of October 20, 1971, a party was held in her honor at the Kahler Hotel, with former students and other community members attending. The following day's *Rochester Post-Bulletin* editorial page gushed about the turnout, declaring "there are darned few people in Rochester who command such respect and admiration that three hundred men and women would plunk down ten bucks a head (part for dinner, part for money gift) to come out to pay tribute to her. When you take into further consideration that the honored guest was a junior-senior high school principal, correctly noted as a tough disciplinarian, this tribute by former students and parents of former students is all the more remarkable....Belva Snodgrass gave this community and thousands of young people who are now adults just as much as any philanthropist could have."

On her special night, Belva was radiant in a vibrant red dress and was overjoyed to visit and reminisce with previous students and their parents. Throughout the night, they approached her and introduced themselves, convinced she wouldn't remember them. However, she proved them wrong, and "with startling accuracy, she fitted names to faces…and recalled incidents often forgotten by the students themselves." In addition to the guests, the Rochester Male Chorus sang "Happy Birthday, Belva," with everyone joining in. Recollections and good wishes from students who couldn't attend were read, and she received a check for $500. According to the *Rochester Post-Bulletin*, several people held up large signs with bold letters spelling out a few of Belva's famous sayings, which included: "Belva's Rules"; "No Running in the Halls"; "18 Inches Apart in the Halls"; "No Dancing Cheek to Cheek."

The party was a wonderful thank-you to a favorite teacher. Not everyone gets such recognition, even when they deserve it, but everyone should get such a party at least once in his or her lifetime. And though the event was joyful, it was also bittersweet. Belva was leaving. But her influence would echo through the generations. She did more than teach—more than administrate. She was passionately involved in contributing her talents, knowledge and compassion to the community. She is attributed with bringing the Girl Scouts to the area and was an active participant of the local World War II Women's Army Auxiliary Corps. She was the first woman to serve on the Rochester Police Civil Service Commission and the Rochester Public Utilities Board and was a charter member of the Ability Building Center. She was also a longtime member of the Minnesota Education Association and the National Education Association. This was a woman who cared deeply for her community on every level. She adopted Rochester as her home and poured her seemingly unlimited energy into every aspect of it.

Perhaps the Rochester High School Class of 1929 provided the best character description of the beloved teacher in a dedication they wrote for her and displayed on the first page of the *Rochet* yearbook, titled simply, "Miss Snodgrass":

> *When the Class of 1929 is widely scattered; when the leisure thoughts drift to reminiscences; when Rochester High School days have receded somewhat into the dimming past—familiar and sincerely admired, the figure of Miss Snodgrass will remain clear in the memory of every graduate student.*

One of the first friends we made as seventh graders was Miss Snodgrass, who managed to know each of us individually, even in those long-ago days. She became then, and has remained, a true, interested friend, giving us of her best thought and effort....A person whose keen and sympathetic mind gave her the power to understand every phase of every complexity. She is the one person, above all others, whom we felt could be entrusted with all hopes, ambitions and perplexities.

We realize the untiring zeal, energy and patience with which she has met difficulties incurred by us and for us. We admire the directness and force of her personality and the keenness of her creative mind. We recognize her outstanding achievements as an educator, resulting both in the improvement of the school and in the welfare of individual students.

But wherever we are or whatever we are, the privilege of having had Miss Snodgrass as a friend, advisor and guide will prove in the future, as it has in the past, an invaluable influence in helping us to form a sturdy foundation for a worthy American citizenship.

At the time this dedication was written, Belva had only been employed with the school district for six years. In that short time, she had already achieved an admired and respected reputation and gained enthusiastic fans, both young and old, creating a somewhat immortal image before the age of forty, a rather impressive feat.

Charles Cudworth Willson and Red Oaks

On a blustery spring afternoon in 1918, a Rochester landmark met its demise. A brush fire, which began with the burning of a large pile of leaves, quickly spread out of control and attacked the city's most impressive mansion. Officially called "Red Oaks" in honor of the groves of trees lining the property but known affectionately as "Willson's Castle," the massive structure dominated the rise of a large hill behind Saint Marys Hospital, an area of land that would eventually be smoothed and graded to make a residential district nearly exclusive to Mayo Clinic physicians and their families for many years, gaining the nickname "Pill Hill" and preserved as a historical district listed in the National Register of Historic Places.

Its owner, prominent lawyer Charles Cudworth Willson, a respected, admired and longtime Rochester resident, watched in horror as flames engulfed his beloved home, a home he had built in partnership with his wife, Annie. Willson loved his home. He and Annie had raised a large family under its steep gables and twelve-foot-tall ceilings; they had hosted hundreds of summer parties among its lush landscape and had been proud to be the center of Rochester's societal scene for several decades. Everyone wanted an invitation to "Red Oaks." And Annie, whom Willson loved deeply and admired greatly, had taken her last breath there seven years before. Her death still pained him. The house was full of memories. He was eighty-nine years old and tired. He would not rebuild. It was the end of an era. Willson died four years later.

Charles Cudworth Willson. *History Center of Olmsted County, From* Enlarged Pastel by O'Brien and LaBeaux.

Located where Fourth Street and Ninth Avenue intersect at the highest point of Pill Hill, "Red Oaks" did indeed seem like a castle to those who lived below its opulent shadow. To some, it might have been viewed as a sprawling example of Gilded Age excess, but others may have seen it as an example of Midwestern success. But everyone in the city agreed it was Rochester's most prestigious and beautifully constructed home. A *Rochester Daily Post and Record* article from March 2, 1920, stated, "This structure was, for many years, one of the sights of Rochester, being stern and stately in its style of architecture and commanding a site unrivalled for beauty in Olmsted County."

Red Oaks was built before the Mayo Foundation House and the Henry S. Plummer House, two of Pill Hill's most prestigious historic buildings. And it was built with love. Not long after Charles and Annie Rosebrugh said their "I dos" on February 28, 1862, Charles purchased twenty-five acres of land, promising to build the house of their dreams. The home had thirty-two rooms heated with steam heat, seven fireplaces, dark walnut woodwork, French plate-glass windows, imported tile, high vaulted ceilings and a circular stairway. It showcased dramatic pitched rooflines and a unique tower. "It is of Gothic style of architecture, or irregular shape, built of brick and provided with Lemont stone trimmings, which are polished like marble," wrote the *Record and Union* on October 1, 1880, "The chimneys, rosettes and medallions, the south center gable and the window caps of the tower are of terra-cotta and add greatly to the ornamental character of its exterior appearance. The roof is surmounted with iron cresting."

RESIDENCE OF C.C.WILLSON
ROCHESTER MINN. 206.

Red Oaks, often called "Willson's Castle." *History Center of Olmsted County.*

Despite its grandeur, the house was above all a family home to Willson, Annie and their children. And when Willson wasn't working diligently in his law office, located in the Union National Bank building downtown, he was found lounging on the wicker furniture of his large veranda, walking the graded pathways of his acreage, taking in the 360-degree views from the windows of the home's seventy-five-foot-tall tower, or enjoying dinners and games with his family.

On that devastating spring day, firemen tried valiantly to save Red Oaks, working from 3:00 to 10:00 p.m. to stop the flames. But it was to no avail. The flames were too strong, and it proved too difficult to deliver enough water to the top of the hill where the forty-year-old mansion sat, overlooking all of Rochester, very much resembling a queen looking down on her subjects. When its construction completed in 1878, after a decade of labor, the October 25 *Rochester Post* stated, "It was a Gothic brick structure, with the modern improvements, and is an ornament to the city," and "we have not the plans and specifications of this fine structure at hand, but from a view of its dimensions, proportions, quality of material and general style of work and architecture, we are satisfied that when completed, it will be the most elegant and imposing residence in the city." The paper also stated Willson was "one of the most energetic, enterprising men in the country and is doing his full share in developing the agricultural wealth of his adopted state."

Indeed, he was. Although Willson was a reputable lawyer and businessman, he heavily invested in the area's rich agricultural industry, owning a 1,500-acre farm in Haverhill Township, where he employed several people to harvest wheat and corn. However, after the 1883 cyclone destroyed much of Rochester, including his Haverhill farm, Willson decided to end his venture into the agricultural business. He sold his farmland and also donated eight acres for Saint Marys Hospital, perhaps with some persuading from his good friend W.W. Mayo. He would then focus all his attention to practicing law.

His law office was greatly renowned, and many young men wishing to practice law competed for a chance to apprentice with him for one to five years, gaining access to his envied library, which numbered in the thousands and was supposedly worth around $6,000. The *Rochester Republican* ran an article about his books in its September 20, 1865 issue, calling it "one of the largest and best arranged bookcases we have seen in a long time. The peculiar beauty of it is that it is filled with one of the finest libraries in the county. Persons wishing an inside view of a lawsuit should just look at Willson's library, and they will be satisfied."

C.C. Willson's legendary law library. *History Center of Olmsted County.*

Willson was instrumental in the training many students who would grow up to become prestigious lawyers and politicians. The September 13, 1930 *Rochester Post-Bulletin* mentions several of Willson's interns and writes about the desk and large walnut table where the ambitious men carried out clerical duties and studied. It was a historic table used in the offices of Willson's son: "If inanimate objects were suddenly to be given the powers of speech, there are two pieces of furniture in the legal offices here of Bunn T. Willson, probate judge, that could spend hours regaling a listener with the student days of lawyers who have climbed to either national or local prominence under the late C.C. Willson, who was, for many years, dean of the Minnesota bar." Many of Willson's students practically lived at the law office and often fell asleep at the oversized table, with one stating, "After studying for a good many hours, I used to climb up and stretch out on the table for a little nap with a law book as a pillow. I told Mr. Willson once that what I could not learn from the books, I could absorb from the table because so many students had used it."

Although many of Willson's friends and associates entered politics by running for local and state offices, he preferred to focus on the business of law and guiding his many enthusiastic students into future careers. But in July 1874, there was a call for Willson to reconsider his antipolitical career stance.

A *Record and Union* article from July 17, 1874, discusses the community's desire for the humble Willson to run for office, the editors expressing their enthusiasm for Willson but acknowledging that it was a long shot, as he'd always avoided such a career. The paper stated, "He is no politician, never asked for office in his life and probably never will, has an excellent reputation for integrity and morality, is fully competent, an indefatigable worker…an able lawyer." True to his word, Willson stayed away from work as a politician, only once testing the waters with a run for a school board office in 1880. He served in the position for only a short time before deciding he'd been right all along: he should stay out of the political arena. It was most definitely not for him. Instead, he continued his storied law career. He defended several cases before the Minnesota Supreme Court and was appointed as its court reporter in 1892, serving for three years, during which time he edited twelve volumes of the court's proceedings.

When Willson died on November 1, 1922, only a few days after celebrating his ninety-third birthday, his obituary in the *Rochester Daily Post and Record* set him as an example of an early pioneer who had achieved the American dream of financial and societal success. He was considered "one of Rochester's most venerable and distinguished citizens," and "up until the last, his mind was as clear as it was at the time he gained his enviable reputation as one of the most brilliant lawyers of the state." In the October 28, 1922 *Rochester Daily Post and Record*, the Olmsted County Bar Association published its recognition of his birthday and a resolution stating, "We acknowledge our debt of gratitude to him as a lawyer, for his part in the development of law and its practices in Minnesota. His high ideal of honor, ethics and truthfulness as a man; his energy and profound wisdom as a lawyer; and his close application to the studies and practices of his profession have done much in raising the standards of our local, state and American Bar." On December 5, the organization ran a memorial to Willson in the *Rochester Daily Post and Record*, applauding his long career in law and his legendary work ethic:

> *He did not seek plaudits of the people.…He went manfully to his work each day. His ideals were high, his motives good. He had no fear, no worry, over censure from others. It was enough for him to know and to believe that he was right and then to act accordingly, without regard to whether his acts were to bring either praise or censure. It was his intensive reasoning powers, and his power of analysis, coupled with his indomitable will to work, which made him the great lawyer he was.*

Willson would've been proud to know he was so respected by his colleagues, as his dedication to the law and the people it served was the driving force of his life from the age of twenty-two, when he was admitted to the Bar of the Supreme Court of New York. Five years later, after embarking on a prospecting tour of Minnesota, he opened his law office in Rochester, where he practiced for six decades, not giving it up until his failing health and the loss of his Red Oaks proved to be too much.

The day he watched his beautiful home go up in flames, Willson no doubt was overcome with memories of happier times being with Annie and his children and was immensely saddened by the realization that a precious part of him and his family was gone forever. Perhaps one of the memories he recalled as he said goodbye to his home was that of September 26, 1907, when he proudly escorted his beautiful daughter Bena Victoria down the large curvy staircase and into the spacious front parlor, where she exchanged marriage vows with Neil Morrison among potted palms, ferns and rioting flowers. Bena was a most exquisite bride, dressed in a pale green silk gown and holding a bouquet of simple white roses. She glowed, bathed in the soft noon sunlight, which streamed through the large windows, gracing three sides of the room. Her sisters and brothers were in attendance. Her parents stood side by side. And the mansion dubbed "Willson's Castle," but known to the family as "home," showcased itself as the diamond it was, decked out in beautiful fall splendor befitting a princess bride of Rochester. It was a happy memory of a time spent with precious family in an unforgettable house that became a Rochester legend—just like its industrious and honorable owner.

Agnes Hogan: A Musical Talent

During the last decade of the nineteenth century, a young girl inspired Rochester with her admirable courage when confronted with a personal family loss, a devastating medical diagnosis and consequential procedures. Her name was Agnes Venetia Hogan, but she was known as "Aggie" to family and friends. She became a respected music teacher and talented composer and performance director.

Agnes was born on October 23, 1881, in Luverne, Minnesota to John B. Hogan and Adelaide "Addie" Moulton of Rochester. Addie's father, Henry Moulton, was a longtime superintendent of the Olmsted County Poor Farm. When John took a position as surveyor for a real estate company in 1892, the family moved to Kansas, making their home in Waukena. Two years later, Agnes underwent surgery to remove one eye. The very week Agnes lost her eye, her adoring father died at the age of thirty-nine. The close-knit family of three was ripped asunder. Faced with the daunting task of being a single mother, Addie moved home to be close to her family.

By the age of fifteen, Agnes had received another eye removal surgery at Mayo Clinic. Her degenerative eye disease, its medical term never publicly stated, destroyed her remaining eye. Afterward, two additional procedures provided her glass eyes. Despite the loss of her sight, Agnes was commended for her cheerful attitude, kind actions, and friendly personality. So popular was Agnes that the city selected her as its 1900 Fourth of July "Goddess of Liberty," and she rode in a special carriage during the annual parade. A local newspaper complimented her on how lovely she was with her long hair loose and tumbling, falling just below her knees.

The fall after her turn as "Goddess of Liberty," Agnes attended her first term at the Minnesota State Academy for the Blind in Faribault, Minnesota. The local newspapers commented on her acceptance

Addie and Agnes Hogan with Ella Graff. *History Center of Olmsted County, Abbott (Rochester, MN).*

Above: Dow Hall, Minnesota State Academy for the Blind, Faribault. *U.S. Library of Congress, Historic American Buildings Survey.*

Right: Agnes Hogan. *History Center of Olmsted County.*

and recorded her comings and goings from school during her years of enrollment. Although it must have been difficult to live away from Addie and her beloved foster sister, Ella Graff, Agnes excelled, especially in her music studies. She sang, played piano and proved she had quite the knack for composing. Her instructors encouraged her to perfect her talent for use as a music teacher, which had the potential to provide a fulfilling career and financial independence. Building on the loving foundation of her family and community and positive support from her educational mentors, Agnes graduated a confident young woman on June 13, 1905, moving home to start her adult life.

By 1910, Agnes was one of the city's most popular teachers, giving vocal and piano lessons. She was also in high demand as a professional artist, regularly making headlines for exceptional performances at weddings and other events and celebrations. Agnes was a prolific composer, creating many original patriotic and religious songs. She directed musical programs at the Methodist Episcopal Church and was a member of its choir. Among her favorite works were the yearly Christmas cantatas, her most acclaimed in 1920. *Adelaide's Best Christmas* was a production comprised of 25 musical numbers and 140 speaking and singing parts for children aged three to eighteen years old. A highlight was a Christmas song with lyrics and music written by Agnes titled "Star of the East":

> *Star of the east, oh, thou wonderful star*
> *Bearing glad tidings to all near and far*
> *Telling of Jesus our saviour and king*
> *Born in a manger, salvation to bring.*

> *Star of the east in thy splendor so bright*
> *Telling of Jesus the way truth and light*
> *If we live nobly and be Christians true*
> *We when may shine for him, even as you.*

> *Chorus:*
> *Shine on. Oh, shine on, thou wondrous star*
> *Filling with rapture all hearts near and far.*
> *Shine in the glory, tell out the story*
> *Christ the Lord is born.*

"Star of the East" was later published and made available to buy due to public demand.

Adelaide's Best Christmas received rave reviews, with one newspaper heralding the experience as "two hours of extra-fine entertainment," and "all were surprised, not only at the excellence of the work of those participating, but also at the originality and interesting qualities of the production itself." The reporter described the premise of the show: "A little rich girl gets an idea about Christmas entertainment for some of the less fortunate and she carries it out to her own and the satisfaction of her temporary protégés," and the "songs, dialogues, drills and so forth are interspersed in a captivating manner, and the result is an entertainment which is far beyond the ordinary."

The Christmas cantatas led to many additional productions over the next several years. Newspapers wrote that Agnes was one of Rochester's best musicians, a treasure to the community, "a musician, composer and poet of surpassing genius" and often "encored repeatedly for her beautiful renditions upon the piano." Agnes created music with seemingly unending creative energy. One of her most popular compositions was "Old Glory":

Fling out on the breezes each wonderful fold
That we may with rapture your beauty behold
All your stars in the blue, your stripes red and white
Make of you, Old Glory, a thing of delight.

Your equal, Old Glory, can be found nowhere.
Let those who are traitors of your sons beware.
We love you, Old Glory, our hearts thrill with pride.
To keep you unsullied, brave men fought and died.

Proudly wave Old Glory oe'r this land we love.
Your designer was guided by God above.
Our prayer is, Old Glory, as years come and go,
Our nation may never do ought mean or low.

Refrain:
Hurrah, hurrah for you, Old Glory.
To our country and to you, we will be true.
Hurrah, hurrah, for you, Old Glory,
Flag of freedom—the red, white and blue.

When Addie died in 1932, Agnes remained at 319 Third Street Southwest, living with Ella. She retired from teaching in 1935 and sold her childhood home in 1949 to the Mayo Clinic. Following the move from her childhood home, Ella and Agnes resided at College Apartments until Agnes's death on October 28, 1955. Agnes died at Saint Marys following a three-month long illness. Rochester mourned the loss of its talented musician at her public funeral, which was held on Halloween at First Methodist Church.

MINNIE BOWRON: ROCHESTER'S FIRST POLICEWOMAN

On September 12, 1910, after garnering enthusiastic community support that resulted in a petition with one hundred signatures requesting the city hire her as a police officer, Alice Stebbins Wells was sworn in as an officer for the Los Angeles Police Department. Wells, recognized as one of the first female police officers in the United States, was a tireless advocate for the hiring of additional women officers, giving lectures to police departments and the public about the importance of adding women to the police force. Six years after her historic appointment, departments in twenty-two states hired women as police officers—a half-dozen changing their state constitutions to do so. Minnesota was one of these states, and in January 1917, the City of Rochester welcomed its first policewoman, Minnie Bowron.

Rochester police with George McDermott in the front row on the right. *History Center of Olmsted County.*

Recommended by the Rochester Civic League and appointed by Mayor W.B. Richardson, Minnie, who was married with two sons, ages six and ten, came highly revered. The January 26, 1917 *Rochester Daily Bulletin* announced her appointment, quoting the head policewoman of the Saint Paul Police Department, who endorsed Bowron wholeheartedly, declaring her "an excellent appointee." Minnie spent several weeks observing and learning about the work of policewomen at the Saint Paul Police Department. The article described Bowron as "a young woman, but not too young. She is strong and self-reliant and possessed of exceptional tact and good judgment. But most of all, she likes the work. In fact, she is an enthusiast. It is believed that in her hands, the special line of work she will follow in caring for the interests of girls, women and children will be effectively carried out."

Bowron was born Minnie Fitzpatrick on February 27, 1881, in Defiance, Ohio. She graduated high school in Defiance before moving to Ashland, Wisconsin, where she married Samuel Bowron on February 9, 1904. She arrived in Rochester with her young family in 1914. As a policewoman, she was assigned a variety of matronly duties, which included working as a chaperone at local dances, arresting intoxicated men who were causing public disturbances, escorting young girls, ages eight to sixteen, convicted of crimes to the Minnesota Home School for Girls in Sauk Centre, offering assistance to women and children to escape abusive homes and investing in the overall health and well-being of Rochester's female population.

Minnie Bowron Tyndall. *History Center of Olmsted County, Cutshall Studio (Rochester, MN).*

Minnie took her role as protector of girls, women and children seriously, and in May 1918, she was devastated when one of her charges was found dead in Mayo Park. Minnie had been made aware of Isabelle Savage, a new transplant from Jerome, Idaho, a few weeks before the fateful evening of May 11, when she was called to the deeryard at Mayo Park. Isabelle's father wrote a letter to Minnie shortly after his daughter's arrival, pleading for her to watch over his impulsive daughter. He asked that Minnie encourage Isabelle to return home. Minnie had done so, interacting with Isabelle several times and encouraging her to move home. Isabelle had worked at the Park Hotel and the Commercial Hotel for several months but was no longer working at the time of her death due to suffering from neuritis, a condition she hoped might improve with assistance from Rochester's medical experts. Without anyone to help her financially or emotionally, the twenty-one-year-old Isabelle fell into deep depression and took her own life. The *Rochester Daily Post and Record* covered the tragedy: "In a fit of despondency, Miss Isabelle Savage of Jerome, Idaho, shot and killed herself last evening at a lonely spot in Mayo Park. She accomplished her purpose in a calm and deliberate manner, by opening her dress at the breast, carefully picking a spot directly over her heart, and then pulling the trigger of the thirty-two-caliber revolver. Death must have been instantaneous."

The fact that she died immediately probably didn't offer much comfort to Minnie, who had to inform Isabelle's father of his daughter's demise. Despite the fact that there appeared to be family conflict, particularly between Isabelle and her mother, J.C. Savage had made an effort to bring his daughter home, expressing he cared deeply for her and worried for her safety. He arrived in the city a couple of days later to claim Isabelle's body. When interviewed, Minnie described Isabelle as "the daughter of a wealthy sheep rancher," "a convent bred girl" and "of an independent nature and wished to support herself while here." And then Minnie added something extra: a warm comment about Isabelle's character, stating, "Miss Savage had an unusually excellent musical education and was otherwise talented."

Minnie's exploits as a policewoman were followed closely in the local newspapers. Among them was a July 1917 incident in which she arrested two men who had liquor at a dance at the Rochester Armory. Minnie closed down the night's festivities and directed everyone to go home. She also arrested seven teenagers "for abusive conduct toward two girls age sixteen" in August 1918. The *Rochester Post and Record* wrote on August 16 that "the complaints are serious matters and incur severe jail or prison sentences if the cases are proved. The policewoman is making every effort to eliminate vice from the ranks of the younger elements of the city."

Under the direction of Police Chief George E. McDermott, Minnie thrived in her position, and it didn't go unnoticed by the citizens she served. A January 16, 1919 *Rochester Post and Record* article made note of her employment anniversary. It said she was "in charge of the work of seeing to the welfare of women and children of the city," and "when Mrs. Bowron assumed charge of the office, it was largely an experiment, but she has proved it to have been a wise move on the part of the Civic League and the city officials, and now,

The Rochester Armory building, where policewoman Minnie Bowron chaperoned youth dances. *Amy Jo Hahn.*

it is recognized that such an officer is absolutely indispensable." In April 1919, Minnie stepped down from her position, passing the torch to Winifred Crossland, who would be known as the supervisor of social welfare.

No longer carrying the public position, Minnie disappeared from the newspapers. Sam Bowron, her husband, appears in the *Rochester Post and Record* in December 1923, being "charged with having intoxicating liquor," and again in March 1924, when he was found not guilty. He died on March 6, 1925 at the age of forty-four, leaving Minnie a widow with four children. Minnie later married Manley Tyndall before dying on January 16, 1956, of an illness exacerbated by a chronic heart condition.

REINHOLD BACH AND THE *EMPRESS OF IRELAND*

On May 28, 1914, Rochester resident Reinhold Bach, also often referenced as Reinholdt, walked the gangplank onto the transatlantic ocean liner RMS *Empress of Ireland*, which was docked in Quebec City, Canada. It was a hot and humid day, sunny with blue skies, and the seventy-eight-year-old eagerly anticipated a long-awaited trip to Germany, where he planned to reconnect

The Reinhold and Barbara Bach family; Edith sits in the first row on the far right. *History Center of Olmsted County.*

with his family and conduct genealogical research regarding his connection to musical composer Johann Sebastian Bach. Reinhold, whose full name was Johann August Reinhold Bach, had immigrated to America at the age of ten with his family and had always dreamed of returning to his birth country. Accompanying him were his daughter Edith and his friends Herman and Freda Kruse, who planned to visit Herman's German mother.

On that late May day, amid their excitement, an air of melancholy surrounded Reinhold and Edith as they embarked on their trip. They had recently marked a year since the death of Reinhold's wife and Edith's mother, Barbara Bauer. Despite the loss of his beloved wife, Reinhold was a man who had much to be happy about. He was a respected citizen of Rochester, a proud father and grandfather and his family owned a successful chain of music stores located in southeast Minnesota.

Reinhold and his travel companions were thrilled at the prospect of comfortable second-class travel aboard the impressive ocean liner. Although the vessel was not as big or extravagant as RMS *Titanic*, the *Empress of Ireland* was still a beautiful boat. Built by Fairfield Shipbuilding and Engineering in Glasgow, Scotland, and commissioned by Canadian Pacific Steamships, the *Empress* had made regular trips between Quebec City and Liverpool since its maiden voyage on June 29, 1906. The *Empress* and its sister ship, the RMS *Empress of Britain*, were built purposely for travel between the two cities. This would mark the ship's ninety-sixth run across the Atlantic. The *Empress of Ireland* was 570 feet in length and 65 feet wide, with a depth of 36 feet, weighing 14,000 tons. It possessed a quadruple-expansion steam engine that powered twin four-blade propellers, which allowed it to reach a speed of twenty knots. Author James Croall wrote in *Fourteen Minutes: The Last Voyage of the* Empress of Ireland (4), "The *Empresses* were handsome ships after the classic pattern of their age: straight stem, sweeping counter stern, two high, raking buff funnels with black tops, and tall, raking masts to match. They swiftly established a reputation not only for speed, but for their steady behavior in the worst Atlantic weather." Both ships became quite popular with travelers and quickly gained a reputation as being swift on the water, reliable, comfortable, spacious, affordable and safe.

Passengers entered first-class accommodations on the upper and promenade decks by way of a main entrance hall, highlighted by a central grand bifurcated stairway made of wrought iron balustrades and dark polished wood. First-class ticketholders enjoyed feasting on scrumptious meals served on dinnerware with a pink and green floral design in an elegant dining room that included long tables lined with round-backed Edwardian chairs and leather booths tucked in corners and under oversized portal windows. The room had hand-carved columns, ornate tray ceilings, cut-glass light fixtures and a circular atrium that swept up two levels, opening to the music room and allowing natural light to filter in through a centered glass dome. Second-class rooms, some of which the Bach party had reserved, were located on the main and upper decks, while the third class bunked below the upper decks, far lower and deeper in the ship. Members of first and second class enjoyed access to a smoking room, library, reading and writing rooms, a café, a music room and a lounge. A five-piece orchestra was scheduled to entertain guests at designated times throughout the day.

Not long after the 4:27 p.m. cast off, at 7:00 p.m., Reinhold, Edith, Herman and Freda, sat down to a formal dinner in the second-class dining room. They ate a five-course meal at their leisure on white dinnerware patterned with a Neoclassical black design with the Canadian Pacific crest in the center. They no doubt discussed their day, the upcoming six-day sail to Liverpool and their journey to Germany once they disembarked. Before retiring, the party may have strolled the outside decks, enjoyed tea in the café or stopped to listen to the Salvation Army Band play. Several members of the Salvation Army were on their way to the Salvation Army International Congress in London. Reinhold and Herman possibly took a moment to indulge in a cigar in the smoking room, while Edith and Freda paused in the reading and writing room to compose a short letter about their first day. By midnight, they were in their rooms and preparing for bed.

Not long after midnight, foghorn whistles permeated the night. A thick fog rolled across the St. Lawrence River, engulfing the ship and making it difficult to see even a few feet ahead of the vessel. Captain Henry Kendall instructed his crew to use whistles, communicating their location with SS *Storstad*, a Norwegian collier carrying eleven thousand tons of coal, which had been visible in the distance moments earlier. The frantic whistle calling was futile. The *Storstad* slammed into the ocean liner's starboard side at 1:56 a.m., puncturing a gigantic hole through which gallons of cold water poured through, quickly flooding the ship's lower decks.

The sound of the collision and the resulting violent jolt of the ship awakened Freda and Edith, who shared a room. Freda was thrown violently from her upper bunk and worried the ship was sinking, recalling the *Titanic*'s brutal end only two years before. Edith didn't believe they were in danger. She tried to calm her friend, but a knock supported Freda's assumption. A disheveled and worried Herman stood in the doorway. He suggested they move immediately to the upper decks. The girls quickly threw coats on over their nightgowns and stepped into the hall, which was then filled with frantic passengers. Reinhold, barefoot and dressed in his white undershirt and black dinner trousers, joined them in the narrow hallway. Since his mobility was slowed due to arthritis, he encouraged them to leave, promising he'd join them. It was agreed that the three would go without him. Upon reaching the open decks, a crushing crowd enveloped the threesome, and Freda and Edith were separated from Herman. Seconds later, the ship lurched, and the girls lost their balance, falling into the frigid waters, holding tightly to each other as they descended into cold darkness.

Unknown to the girls, water raced into the *Empress of Ireland* at sixty thousand gallons a second, allowing no time to close the watertight doors. The water flowed through open portholes, which were, by maritime law, supposed to be closed, but they had been left opened due to poor ventilation. The crew and passengers in the lower decks had little time to escape the onslaught of the powerful rushing water. The sharp lurch of the ship to its starboard side, which caused Edith and Freda to loose their footing and slip into the Saint Lawrence, resulted in the crew's inability to launch several lifeboats. As Freda and Edith bobbed on the water's surface, shivering from extreme cold, darkness engulfed them when the ship's lights flickered and died. The ship rested on its starboard side for a few minutes before the bow rose dramatically toward the sky, creating an eerie silhouette in the foggy night, before quickly sinking beneath the roiling waters. By 2:15 a.m., the popular passenger ship was gone, coming to rest 130 feet below the surface and going down in history as Canada's worst peacetime marine disaster.

Edith and Freda were 2 of the 465 survivors. It was to Edith that *Owatonna People's Press* credited their survival, declaring she exhibited "bravery and calm judgment in a most critical time." The newspaper ran a story on June 12, 1914, capturing her tenacious attempts to stay alive:

Miss Bach, with calm deliberation, reached out to grasp any object within their reach and caught hold of a railing. It was part of the sinking boat, and realizing that the boat was going down, clinging with one hand, she used the other to locate another object. Successfully grasping an unknown object, she released her grip on the sinking boat and found that she had caught hold of a life-saving boat. Here, she clung for a half an hour, and the next thing she knew, she was lying in the bottom of the boat, when for the second time, she was thrown into the water, the large number frantically endeavoring to get into the boat capsizing it. Again, she rose to the surface and caught a rope about the small craft. Here, she clung for a long period, the cold water reaching to her chin, fast numbing her senses. About her, she could see hundreds of bodies floating in the water, some with upturned faces, others not, while clinging to the same boat and floundering in the water about her were men, frantically yelling cries the like of which she had never heard in her life, while again, the feeble moans of others could be heard as they gave up the struggle for life. Miss Bach urged the men to stop

The *Duluth Herald*'s May 29, 1914 headline about the *Empress of Ireland* tragedy. *Minnesota Historical Society Newspaper Hub.*

their yelling and reserve all their energy in the struggle for life, but without avail. After clinging to this boat for a long period, she was helped onto another boat that was turned over.

Upon hearing about the disaster, family members and friends were frantic for news, and the first communications about the Rochester party indicated that all four had survived. However, it was soon discovered that the Bach family patriarch had perished, confirmed by telegrams sent from Freda and Edith. At Rimouski, Quebec, a reunited Edith, Freda and Herman were summoned to the wharves for the morbid task of identifying Reinhold's body. Edith recalled the horrid sight of walking by rows of the dead passengers lying side by side with only their head and shoulders visible, long white cloths covering still bodies. When they found her father, he wore shoes and a coat and had his pocket watch, some money and a few other small items, indicating that he had returned to his cabin after departing their company. Pausing his escape to dress and gather some personal artifacts may have cost him his life. His death was a crushing blow to the close-knit Rochester community. When Edith, Freda and Herman arrived home on an evening train a week after the disaster, accompanying Reinhold's body, it was reported that "a dense throng of local citizens" greeted them home, cheering for the survivors and mourning the loss of one of the city's most prominent citizens. After a sobering ceremony at the Healy Memorial Chapel in Oakwood Cemetery the following day, Reinhold was buried next to his wife under lofty trees laden with leaves in full emerald bloom. Edith, a nurse, was buried alongside them in 1937.

Reinhold didn't see his home country again or deliver the genealogy research he had collected linking the American Bach familial branch to J.S. Bach. He was related to the famous musical composer; they shared many members of the same family tree, including a common grandfather. Musical talent ran in Reinhold's family. An article in the *Post and Record* dated June 5, 1914, commented on Reinhold's musical contributions to the community, "Mr. Bach possessed a considerable musical ability and for many years instructed and conducted a family orchestra of his own boys [Bach Family Orchestra]. As a pastime, he made a number of violins by hand…and he also built, for his own entertainment, a home pipe organ, making all parts entirely by hand." His sons shared his passion for music and enjoyed success in the music business. Reynold Henry Bach founded Bach Music Co. in Owatonna in 1892. Another store followed in New Ulm in 1899. In 1905, R.H. opened a third store in Faribault and asked his brothers, Adolph and Arthur, to join the company. By 1908, a Rochester store had been opened at 222 South Broadway Avenue and was followed by stores in Winona and Saint Paul. Arthur moved to North Battleford in Saskatchewan, Canada, leaving Adolph at the helm of the family's retail business. After R.H. died in 1923, Adolph closed all of their stores, except for the one in Rochester. Adolph's sons joined the business in the 1940s and moved the store to 315 South Broadway Avenue, opening locations in Austin (1956) and Albert Lea (1958).

The Bach brothers were known for their unique skills. Before opening his music store, R.H. had an excellent reputation as a mechanic, repairing farm equipment throughout the area. Eventually, R.H. decided to use his skill to repair musical instruments, leading to his idea of opening a music store. Adolph proved he had inherited his father's skill at repairing violins, inventing a patented clamp to use when gluing pieces of the instrument together. The brothers sold sheet music, pianos, radios, records and record players and found a niche selling school instruments. They also offered piano tuning and moving, instrument lessons and educational workshops and piped music into Rochester stores. On August 14, 1971, Bach Music Co. closed its doors permanently after the family sold out to rival Schmitt Music Company.

Bach Music Co. storefront. *History Center of Olmsted County.*

Time has passed, and few remember Reinhold's family story and its importance to Rochester, but Reinhold was once regarded as one of city's most respected sons, an early pioneer to the area who, "by industry and toil, succeeded in becoming one of the prosperous men of the community, the head of a great family, who, like him, have been successful in the walks of life" (*Post and Record*, June 5, 1914).

Horace and Anna Cook's Daughters: Rochester's Nine Muses

During the late 1800s and early 1900s, Horace and Anna Cook were highly esteemed members of Rochester society. Horace built a reputation as a respected carpenter and builder, involved in the construction of many of the city's earliest homes, schools, churches, hotels and businesses. He arrived in the city in 1855 at the age of twenty-four. Once his craftsman talents were known, he was in high demand, and job opportunities were plenty. The Cook House Hotel and Old Central School were considered two of his masterpieces. Horace no doubt felt great satisfaction when surveying his architectural contributions to Rochester, but he felt his greatest achievement was his close-knit family.

His August 7, 1896 *Rochester Post* obituary alluded to this sentiment by stating, "Mr. Cook was domestic in taste and habits. His life was in his home, and his heart and thought were dedicated to the service of his loved ones." The *Record and Union* echoed this observation, writing that "he was a very domestic man, his happiness being in his family and home." His marriage to Anna Chauncey was a true love match, and he was an exceptionally proud father to nine talented, popular and lovely daughters: Mary, Louise, Sarah, Harriet, Josephine, Ophelia, Minnie, Jennie and Nina. The *Post* wrote that Anna was "a true, faithful wife" and that Horace had "a rare and gifted family of nine daughters, who are all highly connected in the city." When Anna died in February 1917, her obituary commented on how popular she was, that she was a kind and respected lady.

All nine Cook daughters graduated from high school, attending classes in the building their father built, and seven of them pursued careers as teachers. The daughters' social escapades were often covered in the local newspapers, and each married into prestigious families, with several of their weddings being described in descriptive detail in the local newspapers. So enchanting were the Cooks' daughters that they could've easily been nicknamed "Rochester's Nine Muses," and the papers referred to them as the "nine beautiful Cook daughters," with each of their obituaries commenting that the deceased was one of nine Cook daughters, listing their names in order of birth.

The first of the Cook daughters was born in 1858. Her name was Mary Catherine, nicknamed "Mamie." She married to Fred Livermore in 1885. In 1905, two years after his early death, she married Charles Van Campen, a Chicago and Northwestern rail agent. Van Campen, with professional credentials and an esteemed reputation, was considered an excellent match for the popular Mary. When she died in 1910, the March 20 *Post and Record* wrote that her death "threw a pall of sorrow over the entire community" and that her husband, mother and surviving sisters "mourn the passing of one who had made a warm place for herself in the hearts of all who knew her." Mary was a celebrated local watercolor and oil painting artist, and the newspaper stated, "many of the homes of this city and other places are decorated with pieces of her handiwork, in which she excelled, and of which those who were favored with her hospitality were most intimately acquainted."

The second-born Cook sister, Anna Louise, known by her middle name, graduated from Rochester High School in 1878 as part of a lauded class of eleven. A week before the ceremony, the *Record and Union* reported on June 21 that Professor E.J. Thompson of Minnesota State University had visited, conducting college entrance examinations. The professor "expressed surprise at the size of the class that appeared before him and stated it was the largest he had met in the state, and that it speaks in the highest terms" of the local teachers. Louise's older sister, Mamie, was also part of the nearly all-female class (only one male was listed as a member). Rochester citizens were proud of the class and shared in the excitement of graduation night, which was held on Friday, June 28, and packed the auditorium to overflowing. That evening's *Rochester Post* called the eighth graduating class of Rochester High School the "Graduating Eleven." Mamie read an article titled "Builders," where "she spoke of character and of the necessity of building on a strong foundation," while Louise presented "Our Public Schools," which "was read in an easy, confident manner and demonstrated that the writer had a far better idea of the public schools, the ballot box and universal suffrage than the majority of the so-called lords of creation." After high school, Louise worked as an assistant clerk in the money order department of the post office before marrying Charles Herbert Allyn on Thursday, May 19, 1881. Louise and Charles lived in Cannon Falls and Winona before moving to Wisconsin.

Horace and Anna Cook's nine daughters. *History Center of Olmsted County, Crowell Portraits (Rochester, MN).*

The third Cook daughter, Sarah, was born in 1861. Her family called her Sadie. She married George Durand, a deputy post officer and bookkeeper, on December 10, 1884, three years after meeting at the post office, where both were employed. Sadie died on March 28, 1905, and the *Post and Record* commended her for being "one of those ladies who endear themselves to everyone whose friendship they form, and she was loved and respected for many beautiful traits of character." Her death came shortly after the deaths of two of her sisters, Ophelia and Minnie, and the family was devastated by another loss. The newspaper wrote, "She is the third of the nine sisters to be taken by the grim reaper, and thus a beautiful and noble life, whose principal virtue was self sacrifice, is gone from our community forever."

The fourth daughter, Harriet, known to everyone as Hattie, was born in 1863. Hattie was a teacher in the Rochester Primary School System for several years after graduating from high school in 1882. She argued for higher pay for teachers at the primary level at a school board meeting in 1884. In the fall of 1888, she resigned from her teaching position in preparation for marriage. She married George Doty, a successful banker, in March 1889. The March 1, 1889 *Record and Union* wrote about her afternoon wedding, commenting that she and George were "two of Rochester's best-known and respected people," and "they receive the congratulations and best wishes of scores of friends in this city and county."

The fifth daughter, Josephine, often called Josie, was born in 1866. She graduated from Rochester High School in 1885, a member of an all-girl class of six. At graduation, she presented an essay called "The First Crusade." A year after graduating from high school, Josephine was employed at Darling Business College. Established in 1879, Darling Business College provided bookkeeping, typewriting and elocution courses. It also offered a popular teaching program. The *Rochester Post*, on December 31, 1886, mentioned that she and a fellow teacher each received a twenty-three-volume set of Shakespeare's works from their students, "tasteful testimonials of the high appreciation in which the successful instructions of the hard-working teachers is held, are very gratifying to all friends of the institution they have built up." Josie married John Fulkerson, a retail store owner and eventual Olmsted Count treasurer, a position he held for thirty years. The couple was married on September 10, 1891. The *Rochester Post* made mention of their wedding, stating Fulkerson was a "popular grocery man of this city," and the *Record and Union* commented on the nuptials as well, writing, "They are two of Rochester's best-known and most popular young people."

The sixth daughter, Ophelia, was born in 1867. She graduated from high school in 1886 as salutatorian. Her future husband, George Granger, was the class valedictorian. After high school, she taught at Northrop School. When Ophelia and George, who was then an Olmsted County attorney, married on June 26, 1896, a detailed description ran in the day's *Rochester Post*:

> *The house was lavishly decorated with roses of every color, pure white being in evidence. Ferns added to the home a refreshing sheen, and never were the walls of the mansion made more beautiful. The house seemed like a veritable flower garden....A bell of roses, red, white and pink, had been arranged, under which the bride and groom stood while the solemn words were pronounced making them forever one. The trousseau of the bride was beautiful and becoming, being of white satin with a veil of white. The groom appeared in black. As they were surrounded by the roses and ferns, the guests were impressed with the beauty of the scene.*

Two years later, Ophelia tragically died three weeks after the birth of her first child. The April 8, 1898 *Record and Union* lamented the community's loss of a lovely individual, writing, "[She] was a lady of high culture, a charming manner and possessed those qualities of mind and heart that bound her closely to her many friends. Her constant thought for the welfare and happiness of others were a marked feature of her beautiful character." The April 8 *Rochester Post* titled Ophelia's obituary "A Beautiful Life": "A beautiful life has gone out from our midst; a bright and happy spark of light and love has departed to the spirit world, [and with her death,] the admirable circle of nine sisters had for the first time been broken."

Minnie, the seventh daughter, was born in 1869. When she married lawyer Jesse Van Valkenburg in an evening ceremony in 1898, the July 1 *Rochester Post* made sure to cover it, relating, "The bride was gowned in a pretty dress of Persian lawn and carried bride's roses" and said Minnie was "prominent in Rochester's best society and has been for several years a successful teacher in the schools here and at Minneapolis." Minnie died in 1901 of sewer gas poisoning due to defective plumbing in her Minneapolis home.

Elizabeth, known as "Jennie," the second to last sister, was born in 1871. She taught at Northrop School. She was mentioned often in the papers for hosting large parties. Forty people attended one such party in the fall of 1890, with the September 5 *Record and Union* reporting how "all enjoyed themselves to the utmost limit. Dancing was indulged in under a pavilion erected on the lawn, which was beautifully illuminated." On March 12, 1896, she married Victor Qvale, a druggist and respected business owner. The *Rochester Post* reported on the nuptials in the next day's paper:

> *The bride was attired in a gown of pure white satin, ornamented with pearl trimmings, and carried white bride's roses. The groom was in conventional black. Beneath a bell of white roses and smilax, hand in hand the couple stood as the solemn words were spoken which linked them as man and wife. The house was alive with the choicest flowers of nature. Only the immediate friends and relatives gathered to view the union of two of Rochester's most esteemed and worthy young people. In detail the decorations were, for the dining room, delicate pink roses and smilax. The parlor was made beautiful with white roses and lilies of the valley. The back parlor was graced with roses of delicate pink, and the library, where the many beautiful presents were received, was made most attractive with pansies.*

The last of the Cook daughters was Nina, who was born in 1874. Her youthful escapades, which included several picnic outings and a two-week trip to the World's Fair in Chicago, were well documented in the city's society pages. She graduated from high school in 1893, was nominated the class historian, participated in oratorical contests and became a teacher. But it was perhaps her marriage into one of Rochester's most respected business families that propelled her into the headlines. She married Carl Wagoner on June 28, 1899, the only daughter to not have her father present at her wedding. Carl's father, Joseph Hamline Wagoner, was an entrepreneur, beginning his career drilling wells and moving buildings, but he eventually ventured into the music business, becoming a dealer of organs and pianos and a popular piano tuner. He started the J.H. Wagoner Music Company around 1868 and quickly advanced up society's ladder, becoming a postmaster, city councilman, mayor and president of the State Board of Hospitals for the Insane. By the time Carl married the charismatic Nina, he was already running the thirty-year Wagoner business that was then called J.H. Wagoner & Son. Carl continued with the music business after his father's death, but he also bought several buildings, ran a commercial and housing rental business and opened the Wagoner Hotel. Life appeared to be nearly perfect for Carl, Nina and their three children, Joseph, Carlton and Priscilla, until tragedy struck in January 1918. Carl died in his sleep after suffering from heart issues for several weeks. His *Daily Post and Record* January 26 obituary read, "He was one of the popular men in the city and had many friends who will grieve of his untimely death." Suddenly, Nina was thrust into the business world. She gamely took the reins and moved forward, despite her grief. Carlton helped, as did his sister. Priscilla, an aspiring professional violinist and graduate of the Eastman School of Music in New York, abandoned her pursuit of a performance career to help run the family business. Priscilla worked as a Rochester music teacher for several years before leaving to head Wagoner Properties. Then her brother Carlton and Nina died within three years of each other. Priscilla became the first woman president of the Rochester Hotel Association, director and board member of the Young Women's Christian Association (YWCA) and was involved in various local musical organizations. She sold the Wagoner Properties in 1958 and died by carbon monoxide poisoning in October 1959.

The nine Cook daughters and their subsequent marriages were integral parts of Rochester's growth from a small town to a larger city. Their parents, members of the city's pioneer generation and respected community members, contributed extensive time, energy and talent to Rochester's businesses, educational institutions and cultural organizations. Throughout their lives, city residents warmly embraced them, celebrating their joys and successes and grieving with them through heartbreak and personal loss. When Anna died in 1917, her February 14 *Rochester Daily Bulletin* obituary mentioned her lovely daughters: "Of the nine daughters she bore," the editors wrote, "every one was raised to womanhood respected and beloved for the many virtues taught them by their mother. What more could be desired?"

BIBLIOGRAPHY

Adams, Carl. "Nance: Trails of the First Slave Freed by Abraham Lincoln—A True Story of Nance Legins-Costley." June 19, 2016. North Pekin, IL: Self-published.

Barcum, Jill. "Rochester History Recalls a Gentleman Politician." *Rochester Post-Bulletin*, November 10, 1944.

The Black Swan at Home and Abroad: A Biographical Sketch of Miss Elizabeth Taylor Greenfield, The American Vocalist. Philadelphia, PA: W.M.S. Young, 1855.

Croall, James. *Fourteen Minutes: The Last Voyage of the* Empress of Ireland. London: Sphere Books, 1980.

Dieter, Jacob. "From Prison Camp." Personal letter. June 22, 1864.

Dieter, Martha. "Memories of My Childhood." Unpublished memoir. Rochester, MN: History Center of Olmsted County, January 10, 1927.

———. "A Pioneer Woman." Unpublished memoir. Rochester, MN: History Center of Olmsted County, June 1936.

Duluth Herald. "One Thousand Lives Are Lost by the Sinking of Steamship." May 29, 1914.

———. "Rochester's Efficient Policewoman." July 18, 1917.

Eckers, Michael. "The Boys of Wasioja." Community News Corporation, 2009.

Federal Union. "Bailey's Quadruple Show." July 11, 1868.

Flathers, Harley. "Students Remember Principal Belva as 'Tough but Loving.'" *Rochester Post-Bulletin*, May 24, 2012.

Fosdick, C.J. "Lucy Wilder's Bookstore a Celebrated Gathering Spot." *Rochester Post-Bulletin*, May 17, 2004.

Foster, Mary D. *Who's Who Among Minnesota Women: A History of Woman's Work in Minnesota from Pioneer Days to Date, Told in Biographies, Memorials and Records of Organizations.* N.p.: Privately published, 1924.

Freeberg, Ron. "Anderson Survivor Became Area Leader." *Rochester Post-Bulletin*, September 28, 1961.

Furst, Jay. "Indian Heights Has Long Dakota History." *Rochester Post-Bulletin*, April 24, 2013.

Gates, Henry Louis, Jr., and Evelyn Brooks Higginbotham. *African American Lives.* New York: Oxford University Press, 2004.

George, James, and Rhoda George. "Civil War Letters." 1861–62. Rochester, MN: History Center of Olmsted County.

Guthrey, Nora. *Medicine and Its Practitioners in Olmsted County Prior to 1900.* Minneapolis: Minnesota Medicine, 1949.

Hagen, Jean. "Lucy Wilder's Bishop's Bread Is from Austria." *Rochester Post-Bulletin*, May 8, 1958.

"How We Came to Build Our Own Cameras." *Sears, Roebuck & Co. Catalogue*, no. 117 (1908): 672.

Klein, Rosemary. "Marion Sloan's Diary Offers Vignettes of Bygone Era." *Rochester Post-Bulletin*, August 5, 1983.

Leonard, Honorable Joseph A. *History of Olmsted County, Minnesota.* Chicago: Goodspeed Historical Association, 1910.

LIFE. "Speaking of Pictures…Hollywood Has Uncovered Shapeliest 'Shadow Girl.'" September 13, 1943.

Los Angeles Times. "The Daring Young Girl on a Flying Machine: On a Wing and a Prayer, Lillian Thrilled Fans." February 19, 1989.

Minneapolis Morning Tribune. "Father Parachuted; Now His Daughter Leaps from Plane." September 17, 1920.

———. "Police Woman Arrests Men." July 17, 1917.

———. "Rochester Aviator Wins Honors Twice." December 6, 1918.

Minneapolis Star Tribune. June 25, 1901.

Minneapolis Sunday Tribune. "Unique Rochester Is Full of Individualists." February 14, 1960.

Minneapolis Tribune. "The Close of the Year." June 21, 1891.

Mitchell, W.H. *Geographical and Statistical Sketch of the Past and Present of Goodhue County, Together with a General View of the State of Minnesota.* Minneapolis, MN: O.S. King, Book and Job Printing, 1869.

New York Times, 1929. Reprinted in *Rochester Post-Bulletin.* "Hugh Cooper, Former Rochester Man, Tours from One Great Engineering Job to Another." April 26, 1929.

Northwestern Bulletin-Appeal. "Elizabeth Taylor Greenfield." March 14, 1825.

O'Hara, Shirley. "Letter to Miss Herwig, Rochester Senior High School." Personal letter. 1944. History Center of Olmsted County.

Olmsted County Democrat. September 7, 1906.

————. "Driver of 'Badge E,' a Racehorse." October 18, 1894.

————. "Frank B. Kellogg: Former County Boy Now Risen to Greatness Addresses Farmers." October 8, 1909.

————. "The Mausoleum: The Beautiful Family Tomb Erected by G.W. Dusen in Oakwood Cemetery Is Completed." December 8, 1898.

————. "Organization Effected." September 29, 1899.

————. "Reports of Miss Sloan, Vice-President of State Woman's Suffrage Association." November 10, 1905.

————. "Van Dusen Mausoleum: Oakwood Cemetery Is Soon to Be Beautified by a Magnificent Family Tomb." June 16, 1898.

————. "Vote for Mrs. Witherstine." March 17, 1911.

————. "The Woman's Vote." March 17, 1911.

————. "Women Have Chosen Mrs. H.H. Witherstine." March 3, 1911.

————. "Women's Rights." September 15, 1899.

Owatonna People's Press. "Tragic End of Reinholdt Bach." June 12, 1914.

Pioneer Press. "Minnesota Is Home to Grave of First Male Slave Lincoln Freed." July 17, 2015.

Pond, Samuel William. "The Dakotas or Sioux in Minnesota as They Were in 1834." Collection of the Minnesota Historical Society 7, no. 12 (1908): 319–501.

Post and Record. June 23, 1899.

————. "High Noon Wedding at 'Red Oaks.'" September 27, 1907.

————. "Mrs. Charles Van Campen Passes from This Life to the Great Beyond Early Sunday Morning." March 20, 1910.

————. "Mrs. George Durand Has Passed Away." March 31, 1905.

————. "Obituary." January 22, 1904.

————. "Pioneer Business Institution to Occupy Mammoth Quarters." April 11, 1913.

Record and Union. March 7, 1890.

————. September 11, 1891.

————. October 12, 1894.

————. October 19, 1894.

————. August 14, 1896.

————. "An Accomplished Jockey." October 12, 1894.

————. "Board of Education." February 15, 1884.

———. "Col. James George's Death at Rochester." March 17, 1882.

———. "Comedy." February 11, 1887.

———. "Commencement." June 28, 1878.

———. "Commencement Exercises." May 28, 1886.

———. "Convention Closes: The Olmsted County Equal Suffrage Association Effects a Permanent Organization at Its Convention—Some Interesting Speeches." September 29, 1899.

———. "Free Reading Room Entertainment." August 13, 1886.

———. "Hon. C.C. Willson." July 17, 1874.

———. "Hymeneal." May 20, 1881.

———. "Hymeneal." March 1, 1889.

———. "Obituary." August 7, 1896.

———. "A Palatial Residence." October 1, 1880.

———. "The State University." June 21, 1878.

Rochester City News. "Cooke's Royal Circus!" July 25, 1860.

———. "Cooke's Royal Circus!" July 31, 1860.

Rochester City Post. December 1, 1860.

———. July 13, 1861.

———. "The Black Swan." October 3, 1863.

———. "Here and Hereabouts." August 4, 1860.

———. "Here and Hereabouts." August 15, 1863.

———. "Howe's London Circus." July 10, 1875.

———. "News of Our Own State." September 5, 1863.

———. "The R. Sands Combination Circus!" August 3, 1861.

———. "The White City." May 21, 1897.

Rochester Daily Bulletin. June 4, 1914.

———. "Daring Lottie, New Divorcee, Glad That Her First Lesson in Matrimony Is Now Over." April 19, 1924.

———. "Daring Lottie Schermerhorn Is Feature of Celebration of Independence Day Here." July 5, 1922.

———. "Gift For Mrs. Kellogg." N.d.

———. "Herman Kruse Tells Story of Escape from Death, Rochester Man and Daughter Narrate Experiences in *Empress* Disaster." June 1, 1914.

———. "Mrs. Lottie Schermerhorn Is First State Woman to Make a Parachute Jump from Plane." August 27, 1920.

———. "Pioneer Lady Passes Away." February 14, 1917.

———. "Police Woman Now on Duty in Rochester." January 27, 1917.

———. "Reinholdt Bach Meets Death in Ocean Liner Disaster." June 1, 1914.

———. "Republican Delegates Picked; 3 Women on Both District and State Delegations; Vote Given." March 18, 1920.

———. "Rochester Women to Take First Shot at G.O.P. Primaries Monday; Delegates to County Conventions Will Be Selected." March 13, 1920.

———. "State Senate Passes Suffrage Bill 49 to 11." March 21, 1919.

———. "Survivors Write to Relatives, Tell Harrowing Experiences, Mrs. Herman Kruse Received Letter from Her Daughter at Quebec." June 2, 1914.

———. "Women of City Have Right to Vote on School Questions." March 6, 1920.

Rochester Daily Post and Record. August 26, 1898.

———. January 26, 1918.

———. "Bach Funeral Held." May 16, 1913.

———. "'Bill' Furlow Bags a German." September 16, 1918.

———. "'Bill' Furlow Tells of Life." June 8, 1818.

———. "C.C. Willson, Venerable Member County Bar, Dies at Home Here at 6 a.m. Today." November 1, 1922.

———. "C.C. Willson, Venerable Member of Olmsted County Bar, Passes 93rd Milestone." October 28, 1922.

———. "City Names Delegates: Republicans of Various Precincts Choose Representatives at County Convention." March 16, 1920.

———. "Delegates Are Chosen for Two Big G.O.P Conventions." March 18, 1920.

———. "Expense, Probate Court." February 7, 1919.

———. "Finished Work of Two Years: Mrs. Bowron Enters of Third Year of Work As Police Woman Here." January 16, 1919.

———. "Flying with Lottie." July 5, 1922.

———. "Former Well-Known Resident of Rochester Dies in South." October 26, 1921.

———. "Girl in Parachute Dragged Across Landing Field." September 15, 1920.

———. "Kahler Corporation to Open Dietetic Restaurant Operated by Clinic in Rochester Hotel." November 1, 1922.

———. "Knowlton Store Makes Big Hit with Window Displays." April 16, 1923.

———. "Landmark Is Ruined." April 2, 1918.

———. "Liberty Loan Brings Support: Tremendous Interest Shown in Coming Drive by Enthusiasts from Entire County." March 25, 1918.

———. "Lieutenant Furlow, American Ace, Back Home." February 1, 1919.

———. "Many to Take Part in Play: Beautiful Cantata to Be Presented by Pupils Tonight at Methodist Church." December 23, 1920.

———. "Mrs. Lottie Schermerhorn Now Has an Aeroplane of Her Own." October 19, 1921.

———. "Mrs. Predmore Is Instructed: Olmsted County Woman Told of Work in Connection with Coming Bond Sale." September 6, 1918.

———. "New Chapel to Be Monument of Beauty in Oakwood Cemetery." January 27, 1911.

———. "Oakwood Cemetery: One of the Beauty Spots of Rochester—Where Our Loved Ones are Laid to Rest." January 3, 1902.

———. "Oakwood Chapel Nearly Complete." April 26, 1912.

———. "Olmsted County Bar Adopts Resolutions Honoring Life Work of Deceased Members." December 5, 1922.

———. "Police Dept. Is Announced." April 8, 1919.

———. "Praise Given to the Women: Mrs. McAdoo and Mrs. Chamberlain Appreciate War Work of County Ladies." June 5, 1918.

———. "Red Oaks Is Disappearing." March 2, 1920.

———. "Reinholdt Bach Victim of Sea Disaster." June 5, 1914.

———. "Remembered Organist." May 14, 1909.

———. "Sam Bowron, 44, Dies Suddenly." March 6, 1925.

———. "Seven Youths in a Bad Fix: Youngsters of the City Charged with Crimes Against Two Young Girls Here." August 16, 1918.

———. "67 Receive Diplomas in the Commencement." June 3, 1916.

———. "Study Class." March 6, 1924.

———. "Style Promenade at Knowlton Store Today and Last Evening Is Extremely Successful Event." March 29, 1924.

———. "Suffrage Part of Law: Amendment Is Now Part of Constitution of Country; Secretary Colby Signs Up." August 26, 1920.

———. "Ten Years Ago." March 27, 1920.

———. "Touching Scene Seen Enacted When Mrs. Allen Takes Chair." October 6, 1917.

———. "Toys Galore Are Shown in Local Stores." December 8, 1923.

———. "W. Furlow Is a Hero in Battle." December 8, 1918.

———. "What Does Mrs. Rochester Think of Women Suffrage? Asks Post and Record—Local Women Pleased to Have Vote—Most Certainly Will Use It—Have Independent Political Ideas." August 19, 1920.

———. "Willard Furlow Drops Airplanes." October 18, 1918.

———. "Woman Suffrage Now and Then or How Public Women Change." July 10, 1920.

———. "Women Voters." November 28, 1922.

———. "Women Workers Are Announced: Victory Laborers Among the Gentle Sex Chosen from Various Parts of County." April 26, 1919.

———. "Young Woman Kills Herself in Fit of Despondency Friday." May 11, 1918.

Rochester Post. July 11, 1868.

———. January 13, 1870.

———. April 8, 1876.

———. May 20, 1881.

———. September 2, 1881.

———. December 12, 1884.

———. September 11, 1891.

———. "American Sportsman." August 14, 1896.

———. "At the School Hall, Monday Night." March 15, 1873.

———. "A Beautiful Life." April 8, 1898.

———. "A Beautiful Wedding." March 13, 1896.

———. "The City Elections." March 18, 1876.

———. "Constitutional Amendment." October 10, 1868.

———. "Constitutional Amendments." November 7, 1868.

———. "Cook-Granger Nuptials." June 26, 1896.

———. "Cook-Van Valkenburg." July 1, 1898.

———. "Death of Horace Cook." August 7, 1896.

———. "Death of Mrs. James George." August 18, 1896.

———. "Death of Mrs. J.B. Clark." October 30, 1891.

———. "An Elegant Residence." October 25, 1878.

———. "Female Suffrage." March 12, 1870.

———. "The Fifteenth Amendment." January 22, 1870.

———. "In Gala Attire: Store Windows Gayly and Beautifully Attired." December 20, 1895.

———. "The Graduating Eleven." June 28, 1878.

———. "Graves-Cooper Wedding." October 14, 1892.

———. "A Great Driver." July 10, 1896.

———. "A Great Menagerie." July 11, 1868.

———. "The Kellogg Send-Off." October 7, 1887.

———. "The Ladies' Mass Meeting." April 1, 1876.

———. "Local Items." August 3, 1883.

———. "Memorial Day: A Grand Celebration." June 4, 1870.

———. "Miss Sloan Emphatic." January 29, 1909.

———. "Negro Suffrage." November 7, 1868.

———. "Oakwood Cemetery." July 15, 1898.

———. "The Owners of Badge Returned." August 28, 1896.

———. "A Pretty Display." December 23, 1898.

———. "R.W.S. Association." January 22, 1870.

———. "A Series of Surprises." December 31, 1886.

———. "Star of the West." December 31, 1886.

———. "The State Fair." September 16, 1881.

———. "Suffrage." December 8, 1866.

———. "Suffrage Amendment." February 3, 1866.

———. "The Suffrage Question." March 14, 1868.

———. "Universal Suffrage." February 10, 1866.

———. "Women and Caucuses." April 8, 1876.

———. "Woman's Christian Temperance Union." July 22, 1892.

Rochester Post-Bulletin. "Agnes V. Hogan Dies in Hospital." October 28, 1955.

———. "Aircraft Control Base Entertains 450 Guests." May 21, 1956.

———. "Aircraft Control Base Schedules Open House." May 15, 1956.

———. "Air Defense Radar Station Near City to Open in June." March 17, 1955.

———. "Air Force Station." August 20, 1954.

———. "Air Force to Occupy Radar Station Upon Completion." July 16, 1955.

———. "Answer Man: Hotel Traces Roots to Circus Musician." February 12, 2016.

———. "Answer Man: Sears Founder Had His Start in Stewartville." October 20, 2018.

———. "Answer Man: With a Name Like Snodgrass…." January 16, 2018.

———. "Bach Music Co. Plans for 75th Anniversary." September 14, 1967.

———. "Belva Snodgrass to Retire in July: Educator Observes 65th Anniversary." October 20, 1955.

———. "Big Plane Makes Maiden Trip on Twin City Line." July 13, 1928.

———. "City's Airport Named Lobb Field; Plaque and Scroll Honor Pioneer." September 30, 1952.

———. "Dayton Company Buys Knowlton's." August 9, 1952.

———. "Desk and Table Once Used by Men Who Rose to Fame Still in Rochester Law Office." September 13, 1930.

———. "Drs. Mayo Join U.S. Leaders in Kellogg Tribute." December 22, 1937.

———. "F.B. Kellogg Dies; Began Career Here." December 22, 1937.

———. "Ferrying Detachment Here Plays Vital Role in Movement of Planes to the Front." February 22, 1944.

———. "Former Bookstore Owner Lucy Wilder Dies at 79." July 15, 1968.

———. "Former Principal Belva Snodgrass Dies." May 13, 1983.

———. "Granville Woodworth Memorial Gateway at Oakwood Cemetery Entrance Completed." October 29, 1929.

———. "Hugh Cooper's Inauspicious Rochester Start Recalled; Gets Highest Soviet Award." August 31, 1932.

———. "Making Merchandise History." October 26, 1991.

———. "Marion L. Sloan, Here Since 1856, Dies at 95." January 26, 1942.

———. "Mrs. Frank B. Kellogg Dies at Home in St. Paul." October 2, 1942.

———. "Mrs. M. Tyndall Dies Here at 74." January 16, 1956.

———. "Mrs. Witherstine, 87, Dies Here." September 5, 1949.

———. "Planes Arrive for Aerial Show and Port Dedication; 'Speed' Holman to Perform." June 10, 1929.

———. "Radar Base Here to Close by July 1." June 17, 1957.

———. "Razing Work Begun Here by Dayton's." October 30, 1952.

———. "Rochester Air Center of Territory." June 11, 1928.

———. "Rochester Always Builds for Future, Dr. C.H. Mayo Says in Dedicating Airport." June 12, 1929.

———. "Rochester Girl Gets Starring Role in Latest Hollywood Cinderella Story." June 5, 1943.

———. "Rochester Girl, 20, Under Long-Term Film Contract." December 5, 1944.

———. "U.S. Radar Base Here May Be Discontinued." April 13, 1957.

———. "William Friedell, City, Dies at 96." April 3, 1969.

———. "Woman Named to Police Civil Service Commission." April 2, 1954.

Rochester Republican. "C.C. Willson Furnished His Office with One of the Largest and Best Arranged Book Cases: Fine Library of Books." September 20, 1865.

———. "Concert." September 30, 1863.

Rochet. "Miss Snodgrass." 1928–29.

Rogers, James, Grafton. *Biographies of the Presidents of the American Bar Association, 1878–1928.* Chicago: American Bar Leaders, 1932.

Saint Paul Daily Globe. "Badge Was Rapid: Broke Rochester Track Record." August 31, 1895.

Saint Paul Pioneer Press. "Minnesotans: Number of Inventors Is on the Rise." November 1, 1992.

Severson, Harold. "Dr. Lucy Bolt Easton Had Respect of Medical Competitors." *Post Bulletin*, June 11, 1983.

———. "Shirley Went from City to Movies; Now Studio Publicist." *Post-Bulletin*, June 2, 1980.

Sloan, Marion. "Women Deserve Suffrage, a Strong Protest Against Plan to Disfranchise Women." *Olmsted County Democrat*, November 18, 1904.

Stearns, S.B. "Minutes of a Meeting of R.W.S.A Held December 11, 1869." *Rochester Post*, December 18, 1869.

———. "A Woman's Suffrage Association." *Rochester Post*, November 27, 1869.

Sterling, David N. "Photographs to Phonographs: The Conley Story." *Photographic Collectors' Newsletter* 3, no. 4 (August 1975): 1–17.

Stolle, Matt. "UU Church Marks 150 Years of Activist Spirit." *Rochester Post-Bulletin*, April 9, 2016.

Stowe, Harriet Beecher. *Sunny Memories of Foreign Lands*. Vol. 2. London: Sampson Low, Son & Co., 1854.

TIME. "Milestones." October 12, 1942.

Upham, Warren. *Minnesota Geographic Names: Their Origin and Historic Significance*. Saint Paul, MN: Cowell Press Inc., 1920.

Webb, Steve. "Whatever Happened to…Knowlton's Was City's Largest Store." *Rochester Post-Bulletin*, May 31, 1978.

Weber, Tom. "Locals, Stars, Intellectuals Mingled at Wilder's Bookstore." *Rochester Post-Bulletin*, December 21, 2005.

Wilmar Tribune. "Victory Dinner." October 29, 1919.

———. "Women Planning to Celebrate: Day When Minnesota Legislature 'Goes Over Top' for Women's Right to Vote." September 3, 1919.

Withers, Charles, and Robert Withers. "Editorial." *Rochester Post-Bulletin*, October 20, 1971.

———. "Respect, Admiration for Miss Snodgrass." *Rochester Post-Bulletin*, October 21, 1971.

Yeager, Gordon. "Belva Snodgrass Fits Names and Faces Accurately at Sentimental Birthday Party." *Rochester Post-Bulletin*, October 21, 1971.

Websites

Hallberg, George R., E. Arthur Bettis III and Jean C. Prior. "Geologic Overview of the Paleozoic Plateau Region of Northeastern Iowa." Proceedings of the Iowa Academy of Science. 1984. https://scholarworks.uni.edu/pias/vol91/iss1/4.

History Center of Olmsted County. "A Mystery Even After Death: The story of Jacob Dieter." 2021. https://www.olmstedhistory.com/news/a-mystery-even-after-death--the-story-of-jacob-dieter.

Illinois Supreme Court. "*Bailey v. Cromwell*, 4 Ill. 71, 3 Scam. 71 (July 1841)." https://cite.case.law/ill/4/71/.

Iowa Geological Survey. https://iowageologicalsurvey.org/landforms/palezoic-plateau/.

Minnesota Department of Natural Resources. https://www.dnr.state.mn.us/ecs/222L/index.html.

Olar, Jared. "Bill Costley—Pekin's Link to 'Juneteenth.'" Local History Room: Pekin Public Library. https://fromthehistoryroom.wordpress.com/2019/06/15/black-nance-and-her-son-private-william-h-costley.

Standiford, Lcs. "The Circus Was Once America's Top Entertainment. Here's Why Its Golden Age Began to Fade." Theiss, Dr. Nancy Stearns. "A Voice During the Women's Movement: The Order of the Eastern Star." California Freemason. http://californiafreemason.org/2019/04/20/a-voice-during-the-womens-movement-2/.

TIME, June 15, 2021. https://time.com/6073381/circus-history/.

Other Resources

History Center of Olmsted County Library and Archives
National Registry of Historic Places

About the Author

Amy Jo Hahn is a native of southeast Minnesota. She grew up in Harmony, a small rural town an hour south of Rochester. She has a bachelor's degree from Winona State University, a master's degree from Arizona State University's Walter Cronkite School of Journalism and Mass Communication and a historic preservation certificate from Bucks County Community College, where she was awarded the college's Historic Preservation Award, given annually to one student for outstanding work in historic preservation. Her nonfiction work has appeared in several publications. Her first book for The History Press was *Lost Rochester, Minnesota*. She has worked as a magazine editor, a television news producer, an online content writer and a health education writer and editor for Mayo Clinic, where she won several National Health Information Awards.

Visit Amy at www.facebook.com/amyhahnauthor, www.amy-hahn.com and @amyhahnauthor.
Contact Amy at amyhahnauthor@gmail.com.

Visit us at
www.historypress.com
....